SPEAKING ILL OF THE DEAD:

Jerks in New Mexico History

SPEAKING ILL OF THE DEAD:

Jerks in New Mexico History

Sam Lowe

Guilford, Connecticut

*To the kind and gentle people of New Mexico, who opened
their homes, hearts, and archives as I journeyed across their
state in search of their unsavory ancestors.*

To buy books in quantity for corporate use
or incentives, call **(800) 962-0973**
or e-mail **premiums@GlobePequot.com**.

Text design by Sheryl P. Kober
Project editor: Meredith Dias
Layout artist: Milly Iacono

Library of Congress Cataloging-in-Publication Data

Lowe, Sam.
  Speaking ill of the dead : jerks in New Mexico history / Sam Lowe.
     p. cm.
  Includes bibliographical references and index.
  ISBN 978-0-7627-7352-7
  1. New Mexico—History—Anecdotes. 2. New
Mexico—Biography—Anecdotes. 3. Outlaws—New
Mexico—Biography—Anecdotes. 4. Rogues and vagabonds—New
Mexico—Biography—Anecdotes. 5. Criminals—New
Mexico—Biography—Anecdotes. I. Title. II. Title: Jerks in New Mexico
history.
  F796.6.L69 2012
  978.9—dc23
                                 2011048049

Printed in the United States of America

10 9 8 7 6 5 4 3 2 1

Contents

Acknowledgments

My most sincere gratitude to those who helped gather the information, details, and photos necessary for this effort, including Judy Kahlor, Martha McCaffrey, George Oxford Miller, Daniel Kosharek, Marshall Trimble, George Berg, and Victoria Baker.

Introduction

Considering New Mexico's crime rate in the late 1800s, its citizens of today might look back at that time and wonder just how their state survived. New Mexico was constantly under some sort of attack, either by outlaws, lawmen gone bad, crooked politicians, rustlers, murderers, lynch mobs, or gangs that ruled with a form of frontier tyranny.

While Billy the Kid is the iconic figure in any compilation of New Mexico's rather inglorious past, there were many others whose vile deeds and evil doings not only matched but often surpassed those credited to the young antihero.

The following pages are devoted to them: the nefarious and the just plain rotten. Although they were hardly model citizens, their stories are embedded in the state's history, and thus worth repeating. The tales included here are as factual as possible, considering the wide variety of facts, myths, legends, tall tales, and outright fiction that surrounds nearly all the subjects.

Sam Lowe
November 2011

Prologue: The Lincoln County War

Many of the characters presented in the following pages were associates who were involved in New Mexico's infamous Lincoln County War. It is, therefore, mandatory that their participation in that historical episode be considered in any retelling of their lives.

However, to avoid duplication and repetition, this is a summary of the bloody event, so the reader does not have to flip from chapter to chapter in an effort to keep track of all the names, places, and dates.

Essentially, the Lincoln County War was a conflict between two rival business enterprises. Its beginnings go back to the early 1870s, when Lawrence Murphy, an Irish immigrant and Civil War veteran, moved to the small community of Lincoln, in Lincoln County, New Mexico Territory, where he opened a general store. In 1873, Murphy hired James Dolan as a clerk. Like Murphy, Dolan was a native of Ireland and a Civil War veteran. The store, commonly referred to as "The House," was the only enterprise of its kind in the county, so it prospered. In 1874, Murphy and Dolan became business partners. They let John Riley, another Irish immigrant, buy into the firm and formed Murphy & Dolan Mercantile and Banking. As the business grew, the company bought large cattle ranches, then won contracts to supply beef to a US Army post at Fort Stanton and the Mescalero Apache Reservation. These actions, along with farm and ranch financing and substantial donations to politicians, gave the outfit virtual control of all trade in the county. Eventually, Lincoln County became their financial realm.

But the monopoly was challenged in 1877 when John Tunstall, a wealthy young Englishman, and Alexander McSween, a lawyer, moved to Lincoln and set up a rival business called H. H. Tunstall & Company. Because many area ranchers and businessmen resented the Murphy-Dolan grip on the economy, they threw their financial support to the new enterprise. Chief among them was John Chisum,

John Tunstall was a victim of the Lincoln County War.

a wealthy rancher who owned more than one hundred thousand cattle. He invested heavily in the McSween-Tunstall operation. This did not sit well with the Murphy-Dolan faction, which had also acquired political clout by loaning large amounts of cash to the territorial governor and other territorial and county officials. Tunstall also learned that his business opponents got most of their beef from cattle rustlers, but the authorities dismissed his allegations, probably because they were on The House payroll.

Angered at the potential success of the competition, Dolan attempted to goad Tunstall into a gunfight that, he hoped, would result in Tunstall's death and the dissolution of the new partnership. Tunstall declined. In February 1878, the Dolan-Murphy combine obtained a court order allowing it to seize all of McSween's assets, claiming that he had refused to repay a loan. There were two problems with the court order:

First, it was not a certified legal document. Second, it mistakenly included Tunstall's assets.

When Tunstall refused to honor the court order and surrender his property, Sheriff William Brady formed a posse, led by Deputy Billy Matthews, to attach Tunstall's assets at his ranch, located about seventy miles outside of Lincoln. Most local citizens refused to join the posse because, for the most part, they sided with Tunstall and McSween. So Brady enlisted the Jesse Evans Gang, a band of known outlaws, to serve as deputies. To bolster its position, The House also hired the John Kinney Gang and the Seven Rivers Warriors, two more groups of rustlers and thieves, as personal bodyguards. Tunstall reacted by employing several cowboys, including William "Billy the Kid" Bonney, to act as "cattle guards."

Tunstall was herding nine horses into Lincoln when the sheriff's posse confronted him on February 18, 1878. The lawmen demanded that he surrender the horses and sign over his assets to The House. When he again refused, Tunstall was gunned down, reportedly in cold blood, by Evans and two of his counterparts, William Morton and Tom Hill. The murder was witnessed from a distance by Bonney, Rob Widenmann, Jim Middleton, and Richard Brewer, all Tunstall employees. They swore revenge for the killing, and historians point to the incident as the official start of the Lincoln County War.

The next day, Brewer sent a funeral party to the site to retrieve Tunstall's body. They tied it to the back of a burro and returned it to Lincoln, where Morton was loudly proclaiming that the victim had resisted arrest and fired at the posse, so they were forced to kill him. A coroner's inquest was held at the McSween house; no charges were filed.

Acting on the belief that the entire criminal justice system in the territory was under The House's control, Billy the Kid and several other Tunstall hired hands formed a group known as "the Regulators" to avenge their employer's murder. Their ranks were composed of American and Mexican cowboys. The most dedicated called themselves the "iron clad" members. That faction included Bonney, Brewer, Frank McNab, Doc Scurlock, Jim French, John Middleton, George Coe, Frank Coe, José Chavez y Chavez, Charlie Bowdre, Tom O'Folliard, Fred Waite, and Henry Brown.

Before challenging The House, however, the Regulators attempted a maneuver that they considered legal. Although Brady was the county sheriff, the Regulators went to Justice of the Peace John Wilson and had him deputize them. Then, accompanied by Constable Atanacio Martinez, Bonney and Waite went to Brady's office with warrants for the arrest of the men they held responsible for Tunstall's death. Brady scoffed at their demands. He retaliated by arresting the newly appointed deputies, as well as the constable. Then he threw them in jail for several days. After they were released, Brady kept Billy the Kid's prized rifle. Now the Regulators went looking for their enemies in earnest.

Within two weeks, they spotted five of the suspected killers crossing the Penasco River and took off after them. Once the chase started, the suspects split up; the Regulators went after Morton, Frank Baker, and Dick Loyd. When Loyd's horse gave out, they ignored him and pursued the other two. After a running gun battle during which an estimated one hundred shots were fired, Morton surrendered on the condition that he and Baker would not be harmed. Billy the Kid wanted to kill them on the spot. Brewer, the captain of the Regulators, said he would rather kill them but eventually agreed to the terms.

The Regulators and their captives headed toward Lincoln on March 10; neither prisoner made it back. Neither did William McCloskey, one of the Regulators.

According to the Regulators, Morton grabbed McCloskey's pistol and shot him, and then Morton and Baker were gunned down by the other Regulators as a matter of self-defense. However, a popular theory at the time claimed that the Regulators had never intended to bring Morton and Baker to any form of legal justice; instead they executed them as they knelt, pleading for mercy. McCloskey, according to that version, was killed because he was Morton's friend and had opposed the executions. That supposition was bolstered by allegations that the bodies of Morton and Baker each had eleven bullet holes in them and that eleven Regulators were present when they died. Others involved in the episode denied the claim, saying that there were only ten bullets in Morton and five in Baker. Either way, the Regulators declared that two of Tunstall's murderers had been given a taste of frontier justice.

Now aware that he was facing a severe threat, Sheriff Brady appealed to both the US Army and the territorial attorney general, Thomas Benton Catron, for assistance in what he termed "anarchy in Lincoln County." Catron dismissed the situation by handing it over to Samuel Axtell, the territorial governor. Axtell had earlier sided with The House by decreeing that John Wilson, the justice of the peace who had deputized some of the Regulators, had been illegally appointed by the county commission. That made it illegal for him to deputize anyone, which in turn made all the Regulators' actions illegal.

Brady's worst fears were realized on April 1, 1878, when six Regulators ambushed and killed him and George Hindman, one of his deputies. As the two badge-toters and three other deputies walked down the middle of Lincoln's main thoroughfare, Billy the Kid, Rob Widenmann, John Middleton, Fred Waite, Jim French, Frank McNab, and Henry Brown began firing at them from their hiding place behind an adobe wall adjoining the street. Brady, hit by at least a dozen rounds, fell to a sitting position and screamed, "O Lord!" before trying to get up. But another volley felled him for good. Hindman, severely wounded, cried out for water, but when a local merchant tried to bring him a drink, the deputy took another bullet and fell dead while his would-be savior hustled back to safety. The other three deputies—Billy Matthews, John Long, and George Peppin—ran for cover once the shooting began, miraculously dodging the hail of bullets.

For a short time, the street was silent. But suddenly, while Jim French acted as his cover, the Kid jumped over the low fence and raced to Brady's body in an apparent effort to either reclaim the rifle the sheriff had earlier kept or grab some anti-Regulator warrants he believed the lawman was carrying. But the young bandit was turned back when Billy Matthews fired from the house where he was hiding. The bullet creased Billy's hip and tore through French's thigh. Billy dropped whatever he was trying to retrieve, and he and French hobbled back behind the wall. All but French mounted their horses and escaped. French was left behind because his injury prevented him from climbing into the saddle. A local family, friendly to the Regulator cause, treated his wounds and hid him under the floorboards of the now-deserted Tunstall store. Once the shooting died down, he was moved to a friend's house where he recovered.

The body count was rising, and soon things would get much worse.

Three days after the shoot-out in Lincoln, some of the assassins encountered Andrew L. "Buckshot" Roberts at Blazer's Mill, which was a sawmill, mail drop, and trading post on the Rio Tularosa. Roberts was known across the territory as a stubborn loner who preferred riding a mule instead of a horse. He fought with the Confederate army during the Civil War, and although he was allied with The House, he no longer wanted any part of the ongoing strife between the two rival factions. However, he was also identified as a member of the posse that killed Tunstall, and that made him a target of the Regulators.

Roberts didn't talk much, but his associates suspected that he had once been involved in a gun battle with the Texas Rangers. Reportedly, his nickname was a result of that confrontation because Roberts took a load of buckshot in his right shoulder and most of it was still embedded there. The wound so limited the use of his right arm that he was unable to raise it above his hip. Despite that, and despite his part-time job with The House, he was able to work the small ranch he owned in Ruidoso Valley near Lincoln.

However, when the situation had failed to improve and the shooting continued, Roberts decided to pull up stakes and leave the territory. He sold his ranch and, on April 4, 1878, he and his mule rode into Blazer's Mill, looking for the check the new owner had mailed him. Unfortunately for Roberts, several Regulators were having lunch at the mill. They had a warrant for his arrest and, even though it had been declared worthless by Governor Axtell's earlier decree, they intended to serve it.

Once the Regulators spotted Roberts, Frank Coe volunteered to talk to him. He and Roberts were neighbors, so Coe figured he could persuade him to surrender. But Roberts was aware that his name was on a warrant. He also knew about the deaths of Morton and Baker at the hands of the Regulators. He therefore believed he would be killed as soon as he gave up the rifle he was carrying. So he refused the offer.

Back inside the restaurant, Regulator chief Richard Brewer figured there was going to be no quick resolution to the stand-off, so he asked for volunteers to go outside and arrest Roberts. Charlie Bowdre, John Middleton, and George Coe agreed to take care of the matter. The trio approached Roberts and ordered him to throw down his rifle. He responded by aiming his Winchester rifle at Bowdre, and the two fired simultaneously. Roberts was hit in the stomach; his shot hit Bowdre's gun belt. The impact tore off Bowdre's gun belt and knocked him backward, but he was not hurt. However, the ricocheting bullet ripped off George Coe's trigger finger. Coe shifted his rifle to his left hand and got off a round that hit Roberts.

Seriously wounded, Roberts staggered into the mill owner's office and continued firing. When his Winchester was emptied, he took a Springfield rifle off the wall, knelt behind the mattress he had thrown across the doorway, and resumed firing. One of his bullets hit John Middleton in the chest, while another grazed Doc Scurlock. Figuring that Roberts was too badly hurt to offer much resistance, Billy the Kid raced from his shelter to the office. Roberts whacked him across the head with his rifle barrel, forcing the Kid into a hasty retreat. By this time, wounded Regulators surrounded Brewer, but Roberts was still alive and firing. Angered by the unexpected turn of events, Brewer slid behind a pile of logs, cocked his rifle, and fired. He got off one shot. Seconds later, a round from the Springfield hit Brewer in the middle of his forehead and tore off the back of his head.

With their leader dead and three men wounded, the demoralized Regulators mounted up and rode away. Roberts died the next morning. He and Brewer were buried in the same grave.

Then things got really ugly.

John Copeland was appointed Lincoln County sheriff and arrested three Regulators for the murder of Sheriff Brady. All three were later released. Copeland also swore out a warrant for Alexander McSween on an embezzlement charge. It was later dismissed.

Frank McNab was elected to replace Brewer as chief of the Regulators, but his time in that position was brief. On April 29, 1878, a posse composed of legitimate lawmen and several members of the Seven Rivers Warriors surrounded McNab and two other Regulators at a Lincoln County ranch. McNab was killed during the ensuing shoot-out. Doc Scurlock was named to replace him. The next day, four House gang members were gunned down in Lincoln, presumably by the Regulators. Several

*James Dolan (left) and Lawrence Murphy were
the primary instigators of the Lincoln County War.*
SCOTTSDALE CC SOUTHWEST STUDIES

shots were also fired at US Army cavalrymen who were stationed there in an attempt to quell the violence. The Regulators were blamed, and that gave the army cause to side with the Dolan-Murphy faction.

The feud simmered until the afternoon of July 15, 1878. The Regulators, who had taken up positions in the McSween-Tunstall store and McSween's house, found themselves surrounded by the Dolan-Murphy gang. Scurlock, Bowdre, Middleton, and Frank Coe were stationed in the store. About twenty Mexican Regulators took up positions around town. Billy the Kid, Henry Brown, Jim French, Tom O'Folliard, José Chavez y Chavez, George Coe, Alex McSween, his wife, Susan, her sister and her sister's five children, and a dozen Mexican allies were inside the house. Over the next three days, sporadic gunfire claimed the lives of one member of each faction, but nothing approached an all-out fight. It was a stalemate until army troops arrived and aimed a cannon at the store. Those inside the store made a successful run to safety, leaving those in the McSween house to fend for themselves.

During the afternoon of July 19, a Dolan-Murphy gang member hurled a flaming torch onto the roof of the McSween house. After the roof caught fire, the blaze steadily crept into the house, consuming room after room. As the house burned, the gunfire from outside increased. McSween's wife, Susan, ran outside and appealed to the soldiers. They ordered a cease-fire that allowed Susan, her sister, and the children safe passage through the smoke and gunfire while the men inside, including McSween and Billy the Kid, fought the blaze. McSween and two others were shot and killed as they attempted to douse the flames. By nightfall, those left inside saw an opportunity to escape through a back door. The arsonists saw them running and opened fire, killing Harvey Morris, McSween's law partner. Four others, including Billy the Kid, escaped. Army troopers finally moved in to end the fighting. Four men lay dead. After a coroner's inquest, McSween was buried next to Tunstall.

It was the last major encounter of the Lincoln County War. Twenty-two men had died and nine others were wounded. The conflict had settled almost nothing.

But the residual killing went on.

On August 5, 1878, Morris Bernstein was murdered at the Mescalero Indian Agency, where he worked as a bookkeeper and clerk. Since the Regulators were still active, Billy the Kid was named as the prime suspect in the death. One newspaper, the *Mesilla News,* reported that the Regulators "murdered [Bernstein] by shooting eight or ten balls into him. . . ." But the *Cimarron News and Press* declared that "it was positively asserted that Bernstein was killed by a Mexican. . . ." It made little difference to public opinion. Billy was blamed.

After being allowed to leave her burning house, Susan McSween confronted Colonel Nathan A. Dudley, commander of the troops laying siege to the Regulators. She accused him of not protecting her family, persecuting her husband, and looting their store. It did her no good at the time, but she would bring the incident up later, when she filed a series of lawsuits against the army and the Dolan-Murphy outfit, demanding damages for her loss of her husband and property. She hired attorney Huston Chapman to represent her. On February 10, 1879, Chapman was gunned down during a street confrontation between himself, James Dolan, and Billy Campbell, one of Dolan's henchmen. Although Dolan and Campbell drew down on the unarmed Chapman, Campbell later bragged that he had fired the fatal shot.

By the time the war was over, Lawrence Murphy was in poor health and had very little involvement in either the business or the bloodshed. He died of cancer in October 1878 at age forty-seven. Although he became an alcoholic, James Dolan served as Lincoln County treasurer and a member of the Territorial Senate. After acquiring all of Tunstall's property, he died on his ranch in 1898 at age forty-nine. John Riley moved to Las Cruces, got married, and established a hog ranch. He died of pneumonia in February 1916 at age sixty-six.

Susan McSween, on the other hand, not only survived, but also prospered. With the help of her attorneys, she realized a profitable settlement from the estates of her husband and John Tunstall, which she acquired through a lawsuit. She married George Barber in 1880 but divorced him a year later. After that, she turned to ranching. John Chisum, who had backed her husband and Tunstall at the beginning of the conflict, gave her some cattle, and she became a highly successful stock raiser known as "the Cattle Queen of New Mexico." She died at age eighty-eight in January 1931.

CHAPTER ONE

Billy the Kid:
Part One: The Boy Who Grew Up to Become a Legend

Any account of Old West bad men, particularly those involving New Mexico, almost certainly has to include a story of Billy the Kid, whose deeds have been exploited innumerable times in literature, movies, folklore, hearsay, and music. But those who attempt to present a factual rendition of his life must face the nearly insurmountable task of overcoming unreliable tales handed down from generation to generation, biased frontier newspaper reports, questionable sources and, not infrequently, outright lies.

With all that in mind, here's another attempt to get all the names, dates, and places in their proper order, based on well-researched historical accounts, books by respected authors, books by money-hungry writers who wrote the story with little regard for the truth, and magazine and newspaper reports from way back then until the present.

The boy who would grow up to become a legend was born in 1859, according to most experts, but there is no birth certificate to support the claim. The common theory is that the birth took place in New York, but again, extensive research has failed to confirm that. Some findings say he was born in Indiana; others claim it was in Missouri. Less substantive allegations declare he was a native of Ohio, Kansas, or New Mexico.

Many other early details are equally hard to pin down, but what follows is a compilation of what most experts believe.

In November 1859, Catherine McCarty bore either her first or second child. She and her husband (whose given name is lost to history, but most speculate was either Michael, William, or Patrick McCarty) christened the baby William Henry. She had another son, Joseph,

Billy the Kid's grave site near Fort Sumner
SAM LOWE PHOTO

whose birth date is also uncertain, but he apparently was older than Billy. While the boys were still very young, their father either died or deserted them, leaving the family alone in the Irish slums of New York. The poor living conditions—lack of adequate housing, substandard sanitation, inadequate diet, and insufficient clothing—would be contributing factors when the mother was later stricken with tuberculosis. Unable to tolerate the low quality of life available to the family, Catherine decided to leave the city and head west.

For the next six years, from 1865 to 1871, the single mother made a decent living by operating boardinghouses, laundries, and hotels in Indiana, Kansas, and Colorado. She raised her two sons as best she could under the circumstances, providing them with adequate food and clothing and sending them to school. While in Indianapolis, she met William Henry Antrim, a bartender, who became her suitor.

When Catherine McCarty was diagnosed with tuberculosis around 1872, she sold all her belongings and moved her family again, first to Denver, then to New Mexico Territory in the vain hope that the high, dry climate might help clear her lungs. With her permission, William Henry Antrim followed them, and the couple got married in Santa Fe on March 1, 1873. The boys also took his surname, but because his first and middle names were the same as his youngest stepson's, the boy was called Henry rather than Bill, Billy, or William. They all moved to Silver City, where the senior Antrim worked as a bartender and carpenter to support his new family, as well as pursued his fantasy of striking it rich by prospecting for mineral wealth in the silver-laden hills around the community. While he dug and dreamed, his new wife took in boarders. The boys attended school and worked around the house.

But the apparent serenity of family life ended when Catherine McCarty-Antrim succumbed to her illness on September 16, 1874. After tending to all the funerary details and farming the boys out to neighbors, William Henry Antrim, the stepfather, left Silver City for good. William Henry Antrim, the stepson, started calling himself Billy. He found work at a local butcher shop and was considered a good employee who worked hard and didn't steal from his employer.

Then the trouble started.

In the spring of 1875, fifteen-year-old Billy had his first brushes with the law. He stole butter from a grocery store, simply because, he told the sheriff, he liked the taste of butter. Since he had no other black marks against him, Billy was released with a warning and returned to his job. But then he started hanging around with George Shaefer, a recognized ne'er-do-well also known as Sombrero Jack who was considered a suspect every time a minor crime was committed in Silver City. After Shaefer broke into a Chinese laundry and took money, guns, and clothing, he offered Billy some of the loot if he would hide it in his room. Billy's landlady found the stolen items and turned him over to the sheriff. Although reluctant to throw the boy in jail, the sheriff nevertheless confined him to a cell. The incarceration was brief. Two nights later, Billy escaped by climbing up a chimney.

Rather than face an uncertain, but probably minor, punishment, Billy Antrim fled across the border into Arizona Territory. He found work at a hay camp near Camp Grant despite his tender age and soon began frequenting the local saloons where soldiers from the camp relaxed and eased the stresses of army life. Unable to afford respectable cowboy duds, the youngster was forced to clothe himself in well-worn, poor-fitting garb. A cowboy acquaintance called him "a country Jake" and pointed out that he wore shoes, not boots, and had a six-gun stuck into the waistband of his trousers because he couldn't afford a holster.

By the summer of 1877, nearly two years after arriving in Arizona, Billy was working as a cook and busboy in a hotel restaurant near the camp. He had avoided trouble, but trouble came looking for him and he couldn't resist the temptation of easy money. John Mackie, an ex-soldier, had a plan—they would go into business together stealing horses and saddles, then selling them to the local merchants. Like his two previous excursions on the wrong side of the law, this scheme didn't work out well. An army sergeant recognized a horse tied to the front of a local hotel as the one Billy and Mackie had stolen from him months before. The trooper alerted authorities; the two horse thieves were arrested as they ate breakfast. The arresting officer, Miles Wood, marched the pair to the camp guardhouse and ordered them held for trial.

But as they were being ushered into their cells, Billy grabbed a handful of salt, threw it into a guard's eyes, and grabbed his gun. The escape attempt failed. Other guards wrestled Billy to the ground and took the gun. After the authorities returned him to jail, the sheriff ordered Frank Cahill, the camp blacksmith, to fashion a pair of shackles and rivet them around Billy's ankles. That didn't work, either. When the guards came to check on him the next morning, Billy was gone. So were the shackles. But, for unknown reasons, the charges against him were eventually dropped, so Billy was allowed to stay in the area without fear of being jailed again.

As it turned out, that wasn't a very good move.

In mid-August 1877, Billy got into a scuffle with Cahill, who had been tormenting and bullying him ever since his last escape. Cahill was a large brute of a man who outweighed Billy by several pounds, so he had little trouble throwing his young victim to the ground. But as Cahill sat on top of him while administering a severe beating, Billy drew his pistol and fired one shot into his aggressor. Cahill died the next day. His dying statement was published in the *Arizona Weekly Star* six days later. It read:

> *I, Frank P. Cahill, being convinced that I am about to die, do make the following as my final statement: My name is Frank P. Cahill. I was born in the county and town of Galway, Ireland. Yesterday, Aug. 17th, 1877, I had some trouble with Henry Antrem [sic], otherwise known as Kid, during which he shot me. I had called him a pimp, and he called me a son of a bitch, we then took hold of each other: I did not hit him, I think: saw him go for his pistol, and tried to get hold of it, but could not and he shot me in the belly.*

A coroner's jury ruled the death "criminal and unjustifiable." Billy didn't hang around long enough to hear the decision. He fled Arizona, never to return, hurried back to New Mexico and, for reasons nobody has ever been able to ascertain, changed his name to William Bonney.

Sore, cold, and hungry, William Bonney arrived in Lincoln County, New Mexico, about a month after the shooting. He spent a few weeks in the Sacramento Mountains, where he easily made friends, including members of both factions that would soon square off in the bloody Lincoln County War.

Now commonly referred to as "the Kid," Bonney signed on with John Tunstall as a hired hand for three dollars a day, acceptable pay for late 1877. Billy and Tunstall formed a good relationship because the Kid admired his employer, so he worked hard and was considered a top hand. But when Tunstall and Alexander McSween allied themselves against L. G. Murphy and James Dolan in the Lincoln County War, a bloody battle erupted over control of the area's economy, and Billy was drawn into a situation much worse than anything he had previously encountered.

He was loyal to Tunstall, and that loyalty was put to the test on February 18, 1878, when he watched helplessly from a distance as Tunstall was murdered by a somewhat illegitimate posse led by Sheriff William Brady. Since the Dolan-Murphy faction employed the sheriff and most of his deputies, the killing was considered the start of the Lincoln County War. Bonney claimed that Tunstall "was the only man that ever treated me like I was freeborn and white." Because he and Fred Waite were thrown in jail for attempting to serve warrants for the arrest of those involved in the murder, Billy couldn't attend Tunstall's funeral. He then swore, "I'll get every son-of-a-bitch who helped kill John if it's the last thing I do." He was released after the funeral, but Sheriff Brady confiscated his rifle.

The next month, Billy was appointed a deputy in the Regulators, a group of about two dozen men organized to counter the Dolan-Murphy organization. The Regulators captured two men involved in Tunstall's death, but neither prisoner made it back to Lincoln alive. William McCloskey, a Regulator, was also killed, allegedly because he protested the execution-style deaths of the suspects.

Billy's vow to seek vengeance on those responsible for Tunstall's death was partially fulfilled on April 1, 1878, when the Regulators gunned down Sheriff Brady and Deputy George Hindman during an ambush on Lincoln's main street. Once both men were dead, Billy leapt from behind the wall where he and the others were hiding and raced to the sheriff's body. He recovered his rifle and some papers, but had to drop them when a bullet fired by another deputy hit him in the hip. He vaulted back over the wall and joined the Regulators as they rode out of town.

Fourteen weeks later, on June 19, 1878, Billy and several associates were trapped inside the McSween house after the Dolan-Murphy gang set it on fire. The Kid escaped, but McSween and four others were killed. The attackers then let the McSween house burn to the ground. Historians would later declare it the incident that ended the Lincoln County War. But there was no peace for William Bonney, the man now known all across the territory as Billy the Kid.

By that time, Billy was feeling persecuted. He believed he was being unjustly vilified by the accusations of the frontier press and

Frontier Pix

Pat Garrett shot and killed Billy the Kid in 1881.
LAS VEGAS CITIZENS COMMITTEE FOR HISTORIC PRESERVATION

wanted to tell his side of the story. He wrote a heartfelt and well-worded letter to the newly appointed governor, Lew Wallace, saying that he was present when attorney Huston Chapman was shot and killed in Lincoln during a confrontation with James Dolan and one of his riders. He said he would testify against the killers, but only if indictments against him were removed. Surprisingly, Wallace agreed to meet with Billy. Wallace swore that if the Kid would testify against the suspects, he would be given a full pardon. As part of their agreement, Billy submitted to a staged arrest and was confined to a local hotel, where he played poker with his jailers and roamed about town pretty much without interference. He soon realized, however, that he was being used as a political pawn and that, although his testimony helped bring about some arrests, there were no convictions. So he did what he usually did in such circumstances—he escaped and left New Mexico. But then he came back, and his troubles continued.

Less than a year after his futile attempt to put himself on the right side of the law, Billy killed Joe "Texas Red" Grant, a bounty hunter and gunfighter. Grant had openly bragged that he'd shoot the Kid if they ever met, but he apparently didn't recognize his intended target when the two sat down at a poker game in a Fort Sumner saloon. As the game progressed, Grant realized whom he was playing against. After the game ended, Grant tried to shoot the Kid in the back as he walked toward the saloon door, but his gun didn't fire because the hammer had fallen on an empty chamber. When Billy heard the gun's click, he turned, fired, and didn't miss. He told authorities that it was "a two-man game and I got there first." No charges were filed.

But a series of events was unfolding, and Billy's luck was about to change for the worse.

First, Patrick Floyd Garrett was appointed sheriff of Lincoln County in November 1880.

Then Billy narrowly escaped a posse at Coyote Springs on November 23. He and a companion were forced to get away on foot because their horses were shot and killed as they tried to saddle up. They trudged through the snow and made their way to a ranch owned by Whiskey Jim Greathouse. Four days later, a posse surrounded the Kid and several companions at the Greathouse spread. During the negotiations that followed, deputy James Carlyle was shot and killed, either purposely by Billy or accidentally by his fellow lawmen. The remaining deputies fired as many as eighty rifle shots at the house but didn't hit anyone inside. Finally, cold and hungry, the deputies withdrew, allowing the outlaws to slip away into the night.

During a lull in the action, Billy found shelter among friends and sheepherders near Fort Sumner. Apparently tired of running, he wrote to Governor Wallace, reminding him of his earlier promise. The governor received the letter on December 12, 1880. On December 13, he placed a five-hundred-dollar reward notice for Billy in a Santa Fe newspaper. He told the local press that he was under no moral or legal obligation to honor his agreement with a person of such low moral character.

The Kid escaped one more deadly encounter, but then his luck ran out.

He and his gang had been hiding out at a ranch some twelve miles east of Fort Sumner. Garrett got word that they would be coming into town to get supplies, so he positioned his men around an old hospital where Charlie Bowdre's wife, Manuela, was living, assuming that the outlaws would stop to see her. When the riders approached, Garrett stood up and ordered them to halt. They refused; the shooting started. Billy and the others wheeled their horses and fled. All but one got away. Tom O'Folliard, one of Billy's closest friends, rode back to the lawmen and asked them not to shoot because, in his words, "I'm killed." He died forty-five minutes later.

Bowdre was the next victim when, four days later, Billy and his friends had another run-in with Garrett and his deputies. The outlaws were hiding on a ranch outside Fort Sumner when an informant rode into town and told Garrett where to find them. The lawmen then trailed their prey to a rock house at Stinking Springs, near Taiban. Garrett, sensing that Billy would never be taken alive, placed his men in strategic positions around the structure with orders to shoot to kill. The posse members hunkered down in the December cold, while the unsuspecting outlaws slept in relative comfort inside the building. At dawn, a man opened the door and stepped outside. He was wearing a large sombrero, similar to Billy's. The lawmen began shooting. But it wasn't Billy; it was Bowdre. He staggered back inside, but the Kid shoved him out the door. He stumbled toward Garrett with his hands up, then died in the lawman's arms.

By late afternoon, the gang members realized they weren't going to escape this time, so they surrendered after obtaining a promise that they would not be subjected to any violence. Garrett arrested the Kid, Dave Rudabaugh, and Billy Wilson, and they were returned to Las Vegas for further disposition. Eventually, Billy was transferred by train to Santa Fe, where he was incarcerated until late March 1881. During that time, he wrote three more letters to Governor Wallace; he received no answers. Wallace was either in Silver City, looking over his mining claims, or in Washington, D.C., receiving an appointment as ambassador to Turkey.

March 27 arrived, and Billy got another free train ride, this time to Mesilla, where he would face indictment for the murder of Morris Bernstein on the Mescalero Indian Agency. He was found not guilty but was almost instantly rearrested and charged with the death of Sheriff Brady. On April 9, the Kid was found guilty. The presiding judge ordered him returned to Lincoln where, on May 13, 1881, he would be "hanged by the neck until his body be dead."

The trip to Lincoln was in a horse-drawn buckboard. It was far from pleasant because Deputy Bob Olinger, one of the lawmen assigned to make sure Billy arrived safely so they could hang him, tormented and tortured his charge throughout the journey. He would later pay a severe price for that.

The group arrived in Lincoln on April 21, and the Kid was placed in a cell on the second story of the old Dolan store, which had been converted into the county jail. Six days later, Garrett left Olinger and Deputy James Bell in charge while he traveled to White Oaks, ostensibly to buy lumber for the gallows. The following day, Olinger took five other prisoners down the street to the Wortley Hotel for lunch, leaving Bell to watch the Kid. Somehow, Billy managed to shoot and kill his guard, who fell down the outside staircase and onto the street. Upon hearing the shots, Olinger left the other prisoners and raced back to the jail. But as he crossed the street, he was felled by a blast from his own shotgun, which the Kid had taken from the gun cabinet near his cell.

Nobody tried to stop the Kid as he spent more than an hour trying to remove the chains from his wrists and ankles while talking with the townspeople. One citizen even saddled a horse for him while Billy went back upstairs to grab a rifle. One of the other prisoners deserted by Olinger said the rifle was his and asked Billy not to take it. He agreed and went back after a second rifle. Another prisoner made the same claim so Billy climbed the stairs again and took a third rifle. Eventually, he rode out of town, still wearing his shackles. He promised to return the horse; it showed up the next day without a rider.

But the end was near.

July 14, 1881, was about to become a day of infamy in western history.

That morning, Garrett received a tip that Billy was hiding out at Pete Maxwell's place in Fort Sumner. Garrett and two deputies, John Poe and Kip McKinney, rode to the house. It was already dark when Garrett stationed Poe and McKinney on the porch in front of the house and he went inside and hid in a bedroom. Billy walked directly past the two deputies and into the room where Garrett sat, hidden in the darkness. When he realized someone was in the room, the Kid asked, "*¿Quién es?*" (Spanish for "who is it?"). The Kid drew his pistol but never got a chance to use it. Garrett fired twice. One bullet was fatal.

Billy the Kid died instantly.

His life was over.

His legend had begun.

CHAPTER TWO

Billy the Kid:
Part Two: Legend, Exploitation, and Commercialism

Six days after Billy the Kid's death, Sheriff Pat Garrett rode into Santa Fe to claim the five-hundred-dollar reward that Governor Lew Wallace had posted. The acting governor, W. G. Ritch, refused to pay because he said it was "a personal offer made by a previous governor." A month later, citizens of Santa Fe County and Doña Ana County presented Garrett with the nineteen hundred dollars they raised to reward him. In 1882, he also received the original five-hundred-dollar reward from New Mexico Territory.

During his time in Santa Fe, Garrett consented to an interview with the *Daily New Mexican.* When the reporter asked why Billy hung around Lincoln and Fort Sumner instead of leaving for another area, Garrett responded that "he thought that was his safest plan … he was safer out on the plains, and could always get something to eat among the sheepherders."

Word of Billy's death inspired eastern writers, and within months they produced several nonfactual, cheap novels based on their own imaginations and their desire for a quick buck.

Smarting under rumors that he had killed an innocent boy or that the person he killed wasn't really the Kid, Garrett collaborated with journalist Ash Upson to write *The Authentic Life of Billy the Kid,* his version of the events leading up to, and including, Billy's final moments. In the introduction, he noted, "I am incited to this labor, in a measure, by an impulse to correct the thousand false statements which have appeared in the public newspapers and in yellow-covered, cheap novels."

Over the next 130 pages, the former sheriff recalled his early association with the Kid, how they became enemies, and then the rather sparse details about the fatal shooting. He (or Upson) wrote:

> He [Billy] raised quickly his pistol, a self-cocker, within a foot of my breast. ... All this occurred within a moment. Quickly as possible, I drew my revolver and fired, threw my body aside and fired again. The second shot was useless. The Kid fell dead. A struggle or two, a little strangling sound as he gasped for breath, and the Kid was with his many victims.

In the later paragraphs, Garrett claimed that the next morning, a coroner's jury identified the dead man as William H. Bonney, also known as Billy the Kid, and that the body was "neatly and properly dressed and buried in the Military Cemetery at Fort Sumner, July 15, 1881." He concluded the book, "Again I say that the Kid's body lies undisturbed in the grave—and I speak of what I know."

The book did not sell well, but a reviewer for the *New York Times* later wrote that "every story of consequence on the Kid has been based on [it]." The statement appears on the front cover of a second printing of the book, released in 2011. After Garrett's initial production, several others followed. Some attempted to present the facts; most were written by eastern authors with little regard for the truth.

Thirteen months after Billy's death, Garrett met with Joseph McCarty Antrim in Trinidad, Colorado. They talked for several hours, presumably about Billy's death and how it all happened. They got up, shook hands, and parted company, never to see each other again.

In 1928, a reporter for the *Denver Post* was assigned to interview Antrim because of his reputation as an old-time gambler. Unaware that he had just talked with the brother of Billy the Kid, the reporter referred to him as "an old coot." When someone told him of the man's historical importance, he replied, "So what?"

Joe Antrim died on November 25, 1930. Nobody was certain how old he was.

Pat Garrett's remaining time on Earth was filled with disappointments and bad luck. He ran for reelection as Lincoln County sheriff, but lost. He ran for sheriff of Grant County, but lost. He ran for the New Mexico Territorial Senate, but lost. Disgusted, Garrett moved to Texas where he became a captain in the Texas Rangers. Then he returned to New Mexico and ran for sheriff of Chaves County. He lost. However, authorities in Doña Ana County appointed him sheriff to investigate the disappearance of a crime-fighting attorney, Colonel Albert Fountain, and his son. Garrett produced evidence and found suspects but was fighting a corrupt legal system so the mystery was never solved. He was later elected to a full term as county sheriff.

Although many contemporaries were openly voicing the opinion that Garrett had shot the Kid in a cowardly fashion instead of in a face-to-face showdown, he was called to Washington, D.C., by President Theodore Roosevelt. Teddy, who was enamored with tales of Old West gunmen, appointed him a customs collector at El Paso, Texas, despite criticism from his consultants. Garrett did not do well in the position. He antagonized his staff, made several enemies, and got into a public fistfight with a former employee. He was accused of "gross neglect and suspicious dealings" and was not reappointed when his five-year term ended.

The former lawman returned to his ranch near Las Cruces, where he failed as both a miner and a lawyer. Discouraged and depressed, Garrett started drinking heavily and made more enemies. One of them was Jesse Wayne Brazel, a twenty-one-year-old cowboy. Garrett had leased grazing rights to Brazel but became angry when he discovered that goats were eating his grass instead of cattle. The two became involved in a bitter dispute but had apparently reached an agreement and were riding together in a buckboard to sign some legal papers in Las Cruces. But when the carriage stopped so the driver, Carl Adamson, could relieve himself, Garrett was shot twice. He died on the spot. Brazel and Adamson left the body on the ground, drove into Las Cruces, and reported the death to the authorities. The February 29, 1908, edition of the *Denver Post* reported his death. The story read, in part:

*The man who killed Billy the Kid in a desperate gun fight
a number of years ago [had] a reputation all over the West
for his ability to shoot straight. ... He was the most famous
character of the frontier left in New Mexico, having been a
soldier, scout, Indian fighter and all-around gun man."*

Brazel was charged with first-degree murder but was acquitted after a two-day trial. He claimed that Garrett had leaned over to pick up his shotgun from the floorboard of the buckboard. Aware of Garrett's reputation as a man with a quick temper, Brazel said he feared for his own life, so he shot in self-defense. Adamson swore he did not see who fired the fatal shots.

There was considerable speculation that the actual killer was Jim Miller, a known hit man, who was hired by a group of Garrett's enemies. Miller was married to Adamson's sister, so conspiracy theorists made a quick connection. However, most historians agree that the shooting happened the way Brazel described it.

Garrett's problems didn't end even after his death. He stood six-foot-four and was commonly called "Juan Largo" (Long John). Because of that, his body was too tall for any of the coffins available in Las Cruces, and so his funeral was delayed until one could be special-ordered from El Paso. The service was finally held on March 5, 1908. His remains now lie in the Masonic Cemetery in Las Cruces. A historical marker south of US Route 70 between Las Cruces and the San Augustin Pass commemorates the site of his death.

Lew Wallace, the governor who ignored his promises to Billy, fared considerably better than most of those involved in the life and death of Billy the Kid.

After reneging on his verbal promise to pardon the Kid in return for his testimony in a murder case, Wallace told a reporter, "I can't see how a fellow like him should expect any clemency from me." Wallace was never happy about his appointment to the territory's highest political office, once commenting that "every calculation based on experience elsewhere fails in New Mexico."

His wife, Susan, shared his feelings about the territory. In a letter to one of her sons, she recommended that the United States force Mexico to take it back.

But Wallace's time in New Mexico wasn't a complete waste. During his tenure, he wrote *Ben Hur: A Tale of Christ,* which became a best seller and has twice been made into a movie. After leaving New Mexico Territory, Wallace was appointed ambassador to Turkey.

In 2010, nearly 120 years after Billy's death, another New Mexico governor denied his request for clemency. Governor Bill Richardson had considered pardoning the Kid since 2003 but didn't make the call. "The romanticism appealed to me, to issue a pardon," he said, "but the facts and the evidence did not support it, and I've got to be responsible, especially when a governor is issuing a pardon."

Descendants of Governor Wallace and Sheriff Garrett expressed outrage that Richardson would even consider a pardon and vociferously opposed the action on the grounds that it would be demeaning to their ancestors' names.

Like almost everything else associated with him, the only known and authenticated photograph of Billy was the subject of a lengthy controversy. The photo, a two-by-three-inch ferrotype taken by an unknown photographer around 1879, shows Billy holding a rifle while wearing a six-gun strapped to his left hip. This led to the belief that he was left-handed.

But ferrotypes of that time were mirror images, printed in reverse of the way the subjects were actually posed. The photo was the subject of intense examination in the late 1980s. After studying the types of the rifle and pistol shown, the experts concluded that Billy was right-handed. Years before those studies, however, Columbia Pictures made a Billy the Kid movie entitled *The Left-Handed Gun*. Paul Newman played Billy.

After Billy's death, Dan Dedrick, one of his associates, claimed the photo and passed it down through his family. It eventually wound up in the hands of Dedrick descendants Stephen and Art Upham, who made it public in the 1980s. They lent it to the Lin-

A large poster hangs in the Billy the Kid Museum in Fort Sumner.
SAM LOWE PHOTO

coln County Heritage Trust Museum for several years, then withdrew it and put it up for auction. In June 2011, billionaire Bill
Koch purchased it for $2.3 million during an auction in Denver.

The young outlaw's legend got a major theatrical boost in 1903
when Walter Wood's stage play, *Billy the Kid,* received high praise
and public acclaim. Movie producers took notice.

The first Billy the Kid movie was *Billy the Kid,* released in 1911. It starred Tefft Johnson. The next was *Billy the Bandit,* released in 1916 and featuring Billy Mason. The first Kid talkie was *Billy the Kid* in 1930 with Johnny Mack Brown in the title role.

Since then, an estimated forty-five movies have dealt with the subject. However, according to the proprietors of the Billy the Kid Museum in Fort Sumner, the total is probably closer to 150 if foreign versions are included. The vast majority feature Billy as a leading man but have nothing to do with his actual life. In them, he fights bad guys, rescues maidens, and always survives so he can ride off into the sunset. The list includes such less-than-classics as *Billy the Kid's Smoking Guns, Son of Billy the Kid, I Shot Billy the Kid,* and *Billy the Kid vs. Dracula.*

Besides Johnson, Mason, Newman, and Brown, other actors who have portrayed Billy include Roy Rogers, Bob Steele, Buster Crabbe, Gordon Demain, George Baxter, Audie Murphy, Scott Brady, Tyler McDuff, Nick Adams, Anthony Dexter, Chuck Courtney, Geoffrey Deuel, Michael J. Pollard, Kris Kristofferson, and Emilio Estevez.

One of the more noteworthy attempts was the Howard Hughes production of *The Outlaw,* which starred Jack Buetel as Billy and a buxom Jane Russell as his girlfriend. The movie was condemned by the Legion of Decency and other religious movie rating groups because Miss Russell showed too much cleavage. Today, it would hardly get a PG rating.

After movies and books converted Billy into a folk hero, it was only natural that songs about him would follow, and so they did. Aaron Copland wrote a ballet (*Billy the Kid,* 1938). Bob Dylan's album *Pat Garrett and Billy the Kid* was the soundtrack for a 1973 movie. Marty Robbins sang Billy songs on his albums *Gunfighter Ballads and Trail Songs Volume 3* and *Return of the Gunfighter.*

Jon Bon Jovi's album *Blaze of Glory* featured the song "Billy Get Your Gun." Billy Joel's 1973 album *Piano Man* included "The Ballad of Billy the Kid," and the Charlie Daniels Band recorded "Billy the Kid" for its 1976 album *High Lonesome.*

The Collected Works of Billy the Kid, a 1970 play by Michael Ondaatje, featured a score written by Mark Nichols. Others who sang about the Kid included Woody Guthrie, Ry Cooder, Billy Dean, and the Two Gallants band.

And in 2010, an emo/screamo band named William Bonney released its first EP album.

Although a less-than-reliable frontier press credited Billy with killing as many as twenty-one men, he was actually solely responsible for only four deaths. They were Frank "Windy" Cahill (self-defense), Joe Grant (self-defense), and James Bell and Bob Olinger (gunned down during his last jailbreak). He was on the scene when at least five others died of gunshot wounds, but he wasn't the only one shooting at the time.

And, although history and several eyewitnesses would support Garrett's version of Billy's demise, speculation and rumors that Billy lived to tell about it won't die.

Around the turn of the twentieth century, a mystery man known only as Walkalong Smith showed up in the Santa Fe area. He earned a meager living teaching ranchers' children and spent considerable time browsing in the local library. Those who knew him said he was a gentle man who loved animals and children but hated guns.

After his death in 1937, some ranchers who had befriended him claimed that Smith was actually Billy the Kid. They said he had confided in them but swore them to secrecy. According to the wanderer's story, Governor Wallace, Sheriff Garrett, and he, as Billy the Kid, devised an elaborate plot that would allow the Kid to escape. Smith claimed that Garrett and Wallace realized that he, as Billy, had been forced into a gunslinger's life by circumstances beyond his control and deserved a second chance.

So on the night of July 14, 1881, Garrett staged a fake shoot-out, let the Kid escape through a back door, and then buried two sacks of sand instead. The claims didn't receive much attention, primarily because the ranchers who made them could offer no substantive proof.

Then Brushy Bill Roberts came forth.

In 1950, William Morrison, a Texas paralegal, and Ollie Roberts, an elderly man from central Texas, held a meeting with Governor Thomas J. Mabry of New Mexico. During the meeting, Roberts claimed he was Billy the Kid and asked the governor to pardon him.

His claim was supported by a number of people who had actually known the Kid. They positively identified Roberts as Billy, pointing out the similar eye color and several matching scars. But others, including his own relatives, disputed his claims and noted that according to family records, Roberts would have been only two years old when Billy was killed. Roberts had also boasted to those who would listen that he rode with Jesse James and his gang. Then he told Morrison that he would tell the truth about how he escaped Garrett's bullets in exchange for a full pardon.

But when he could not even remember Garrett's name during the meeting with the governor, Brushy Bill's request was denied. He died in 1950; the stone marker on his grave in Hamilton, Texas, contains a line that says "A.K.A. Billy the Kid."

In 2005, former Lincoln County sheriff Tom Sullivan and former Capitan, New Mexico, mayor Steve Sederwall dug up the bones of John Miller and the remains of the man buried next to him in the Pioneers' Home Cemetery in Prescott, Arizona. They said they were trying to determine whether Billy the Kid was really the man buried at Fort Sumner and if Garrett really killed him.

They also wanted to open Billy's grave at Fort Sumner, the grave of his mother at Silver City, and the graves of men who claimed to be Billy, including Miller. But the courts prevented them from digging in New Mexico. They selected Miller's grave because, while living as a rancher near Ramah, New Mexico, he frequently claimed to be Billy, usually after he had been drinking. After retrieving his remains, the men said they compared his DNA with DNA they said they recovered from blood stains at the house where the Kid and Garrett had their final confrontation. The tests were inconclusive.

Miller died at the Prescott home in 1937. So did William Hudspeth, whose remains occupied the cemetery space next to Miller's. His bones were dug up because the graves were not well

*Sign at the
Billy the Kid
Scenic Byway
Visitors Center
in Ruidoso*
SAM LOWE PHOTO

marked and the two investigators wanted to make sure they got the right body. County officials first considered prosecuting the pair but decided against it when they learned they had been given permission to exhume the bodies.

In direct contradiction to such claims, historical accounts state that twenty-eight witnesses viewed the body after the shooting, and all agreed that it was Billy's. Among them was Jesus Silva, who helped with the burial. In 1937, when asked about the rumors that Billy might still be alive, Silva responded: "That may be the rumor, my boy, but if there are dead men in this world, then Billy the Kid is among them. I know he's dead and as far as I know, I am the only one yet living who saw him in death."

Deluvina Maxwell, one of Billy's many friends, was also there. She later declared: "He [Garrett] was afraid to go back to the room to make sure of whom he had shot. I went in and was the first to discover that they had killed my little boy. I hated those men and am glad that I have lived long enough to see them all dead and buried."

Vicente Otero, a Fort Sumner resident, helped dig the Kid's grave. Years later, he said, "I was at Fort Sumner the night Billy the Kid was killed. I went to the carpenter's shop and stood at the wake all that night. Jesus Silva made a wooden box, which served as the coffin for the Kid. The next day, Silva and I dug the Kid's grave and buried the body in the old graveyard."

But Billy the Kid lives on in other ways.

His grave at old Fort Sumner is a popular tourist attraction. It's on Billy the Kid Road. And current editions of the *New Mexico Vacation Guide* contain a section entitled "Billy the Kid's Stomping Grounds."

Billy the Kid references are common throughout the state. The plaque adjacent to a bronze statue of famed cattleman John Chisum in Roswell notes that Chisum was a member of the committee that hired Pat Garrett to get rid of the Kid. Dowlin's Historic Old Mill in Ruidoso was "reported to be a hangout of Billy the Kid." There's a Billy the Kid Springs in Chaves County, and the annual Old Lincoln Days includes a reenactment of his last escape.

The Casa de Patron, a former bed and breakfast in the Rio Bonito Valley, claimed the Kid once slept there. The former Mesilla courthouse where Billy was tried for murder now houses a souvenir store named the Billy the Kid Gift Shop that sells such items as Billy the Kid cups, Billy the Kid key chains, and Billy the Kid bubble gum. For a quarter, visitors can have their fortunes told by a Billy the Kid torso inside a glass case. During a 2009 Billy the Kid exhibition in the Albuquerque Museum of Art and History, guests were asked to vote on whether Billy should be pardoned. The vote was more than two to one in his favor.

Images of Billy are preserved in tile and a wooden cutout at the Ruidoso Downs Visitor Center, and in the neon sign in front of Ruidoso Downs racetrack. Also in Ruidoso Downs, a replica of the Lincoln County Courthouse has been created inside the Billy the Kid Casino.

The Billy the Kid Museum in Fort Sumner houses an estimated sixty thousand Billy the Kid relics and objects related to the young outlaw. Among them are his rifle, chaps, and spurs and printed articles about men who claimed they knew the Kid, helped bury the Kid, and hid the Kid. And, as a matter of convenience, the Billy the Kid Country Inn is right across the street from the museum.

The Billy the Kid Scenic Byway starts at the Billy the Kid Scenic Byway Visitor Center in Ruidoso Downs and loops through Hondo, Lincoln, Fort Stanton, Capitan, and Ruidoso. The byway is marked by signs bearing Billy's likeness.

CHAPTER THREE

Charlie Bowdre and Tom O'Folliard:
Billy's Pals Met Similar Fates

Charlie Bowdre and Tom O'Folliard shared several things in common. They were both cowboys who frequently supplemented their income by rustling cattle. They both fought on the losing side in the Lincoln County War. They were both friends of Billy the Kid. They both died of gunshot wounds.

Their relationships with the Kid were directly responsible for their deaths. They died within four days of each other, during gunfights with posses led by Sheriff Pat Garrett, who may have fired both fatal blasts. They were buried side by side.

Like most, their early days gave no indication that they would choose a life of crime. And, like so many who chose that profession, their lives ended when they were quite young.

They also had similar backgrounds.

Bowdre was born in Georgia in 1848, but his parents moved to Mississippi and became farmers when he was three years old. He stayed on the farm until his teen years, then left and started wandering the Southwest. O'Folliard was a native Texan, born in 1858, but his parents moved to Mexico, where they died of smallpox while he was still an infant. An uncle brought him back to his ranch in Texas, and he stayed there until he was nineteen. Then he left home and began wandering the Southwest.

Eventually, they both wound up in Lincoln County.

Shortly after his arrival there in 1874, Bowdre befriended Josiah "Doc" Scurlock, and the two went into business together, opening a cheese factory. Scurlock was also a part-time lawman, and Bowdre frequently joined him as a posse member. They pursued and captured cattle rustlers, and often were involved when the suspected thieves were lynched in the twisted form of frontier justice that was prevalent at the time. One July night in 1876, they were part of a mob that stormed the Lincoln jail to release a rustler. They took him outside of town and hanged him. Typical of the times, no charges were ever filed. But about a year later, Bowdre and a companion were arrested in Lincoln for getting drunk and shooting up the town.

The cheese business wasn't successful, but Bowdre secured a loan from Lincoln businessmen Lawrence Murphy and James Dolan and bought a small ranch in the area. Later, though, he would be on opposite sides of the Murphy-Dolan outfit during the Lincoln County War. Unable to repay the loan, however, he soon lost the ranch. So he found work on various spreads in Lincoln County.

When the war broke out in 1878, Bowdre sided with the faction headed by John Tunstall and Alexander McSween, bitter foes of the Murphy-Dolan gang. This put him on the same side as Billy the Kid, who had joined the Regulators to avenge the murder of Tunstall, his benefactor and friend.

Tom O'Folliard arrived in Lincoln County in 1878, accompanied by James Woodland, a boyhood pal. Unable to find legitimate work, the pair turned to cattle rustling. When the war started, Woodland left the territory, but O'Folliard was quick to align himself with the Regulators. He became close friends with Billy, and the Kid taught him how to shoot a rifle and a pistol, boasting that he could "make a real soldier out of the fellow." The two were inseparable, with Tom acting almost as the Kid's servant. He held the horses outside while Billy gambled and caroused in the saloons, and rode with him when they confiscated other peoples' livestock.

Billy rewarded the loyalty on at least one occasion. After the Lincoln County War ended, the two were in a gang of ex-Regulators who raided a Lincoln area ranch and made off with more than one hundred fifty cows and fifteen horses. They drove the livestock to Tascosa, Texas, where O'Folliard got into a dispute with a local cowhand over a card game. The two came close to a shoot-out before Billy intervened and settled things down without any gunfire.

*Charlie Bowdre and Tom O'Folliard are
buried next to Billy the Kid near Fort Sumner.*
SAM LOWE PHOTO

Although they were both members of the Regulators, Bowdre
and O'Folliard were not always involved in the same skirmishes.
Bowdre was there when William Morton, Frank Baker, and William McCloskey were murdered along Blackwater Creek in
March 1878. McCloskey was a Regulator; Morton and Baker were
accused of murdering Tunstall. Once the Regulators captured
them, their stated intent was to take them back to Lincoln so they
could stand trial. But somewhere along the way, all three were
shot and killed. A variety of explanations followed. One version
said that Morton and Baker disarmed and killed McCloskey, then
were gunned down when they tried to escape. A more common

theory was that Morton and Baker were doomed from the beginning and that, when McCloskey tried to intervene, he also took a Regulator bullet.

Less than a month later, Bowdre and nine other Regulators, including the Kid, rode into Blazer's Mill, a small stopping-off point on the road to Tularosa and Mesilla. They put their horses in a corral and asked for a meal. As they waited for their food, Buckshot Roberts rode up and dismounted. One of the Regulators recognized him and said he had a warrant charging Roberts with involvement in Tunstall's death. Because they were deputized, the Regulators attempted to persuade him to surrender. The talks were futile, so Bowdre organized a smaller group determined to end the stalemate. They ordered Roberts to drop his rifle and throw up his hands. Instead, Roberts began shooting.

His first bullet hit Bowdre's gun belt, knocking the belt off Bowdre and Bowdre off his feet. Bowdre fired at the same time and hit Roberts in the midsection. Although mortally wounded, Roberts managed to kill one Regulator and wound three others, including the Kid. Bowdre would later be charged with firing the fatal bullet.

O'Folliard also came in for a major share of the action. He was there on July 19, 1878, when he and Billy, along with ten other men, were trapped inside McSween's house after the Murphy-Dolan gang set it on fire. The blaze was the culmination of a five-day gunfight between the rival outfits, with a dozen men and two women caught inside the house. As the fire roared, O'Folliard and Billy led three of their companions out a back door in an attempt to draw the gunfire away from McSween and three others. As they raced toward a gate, a bullet felled Harvey Morris, McSween's young law partner. O'Folliard knelt beside him and tried to help, but it was too late. After taking a rifle shot to his shoulder, O'Folliard fled with the others.

McSween was not so fortunate. He and the men with him were riddled with bullets, fired by a line of gunmen hiding behind a low adobe wall. All died instantly. The incident was considered the last act of the Lincoln County War. The Murphy-Dolan combine had won.

But it wasn't completely over. At least, not for Billy and his two cronies.

Once the fighting stopped, they returned to their old ways. They started rustling cattle, this time from the herds owned by John Chisum, who had been a partner in the Tunstall-McSween operation. Since nobody had paid them for their involvement in the conflict, and since Chisum was the only remaining partner, Billy figured it was up to Chisum to settle up. When he refused, he started losing cattle. The trio figured that each cow they stole chipped five dollars off the sum Chisum allegedly owed them.

They stayed at it for a couple of years, but by 1880, Bowdre was ready to quit the life of crime and settle down with his new wife, Manuela. He became foreman at Tom Yerby's ranch in the Fort Sumner area and then acquired part ownership. He also secretly met with Sheriff Pat Garrett to discuss the possibility of exoneration for his part in Buckshot Roberts's death. They met in early December 1880, on a road a couple of miles south of Fort Sumner. Garrett showed Bowdre a letter from Captain Joseph C. Lea, a prominent business-man, which stated that if Bowdre would "forsake his disreputable associates, every effort will be made by good citizens" to let him turn his life around and become an accepted member of society.

Bowdre promised to quit hanging around with the Kid and his associates, but he reminded Garrett that he had some sort of moral obligation to feed and shelter them if (or when) they came to the ranch. Garrett responded with a warning that if Bowdre didn't quit the gang and change his ways, he most certainly would wind up in a cemetery plot because he and his fellow lawmen would hound them until they were taken, dead or alive.

Actually, Garrett had neither the power nor the intention to accept the offer because a federal warrant for Bowdre's arrest superseded any agreement he (Garrett) might have made. Bow-dre later wrote to Captain Lea, informing him that Billy told him that he would leave the territory soon, and that once he was gone, Bowdre would "let every man do his own fighting, so far as I am concerned, and I will do my own."

None of his efforts brought him any assurance that he would be welcomed into "polite society," so Bowdre left his wife in Fort Sumner and rejoined the Kid's gang of former Regulators.

O'Folliard also wanted to leave the gang. He asked Billy to accompany him back to Texas so he could see his grandmother. The Kid agreed to make the trip, but they never got there. The night of December 19, 1880, happened first.

Mistakenly assuming that they were safe for a while, Billy and four friends, including O'Folliard and Bowdre, rode into Fort Sumner to acquire supplies. But their confidence was misplaced. One of Garrett's men had spotted them as they neared the town. He alerted the lawman, who had enough time to set a trap. Garrett correctly figured they would stop at Bowdre's home, located in an old hospital, so he had his men take up positions in and around the building. Those inside started a poker game while they waited; those outside shivered in the December cold.

Around 8 p.m., they spotted five horsemen riding toward the hospital through the cold winter's evening. Two of them got close to the building; the other three held back. When the leading pair got within shouting distance, Garrett strode out onto the hospital veranda, cocked his rifle, and ordered them to halt, throw their hands over their heads, and dismount. Although surprised, Billy and three others had enough sense to wheel their horses and flee into the night amid a volley of rifle shots from the lawmen.

But O'Folliard, true to his character, turned to fight. He drew his six-gun and began blazing away while Garrett and Deputy Lon Chambers fired simultaneously. The peacekeepers heard screams but couldn't tell in the darkness which outlaw they had wounded, so they kept shooting. Within minutes, one of the riders slowed down and turned his horse toward the posse. With a row of rifle barrels aimed at his body, he approached the lawmen while his comrades fled into the night. It was Tom O'Folliard. A slug had pierced his left side, just below his heart. The pain was too great; he had no chance of escape. After dropping his pistol, he walked his horse slowly back to the lawmen and winced, "Don't shoot anymore! I'm killed!"

The twenty-two-year-old outlaw fell off his mount, into the arms of the posse members. They carried him inside the old hospital and laid him on the floor. He requested that they let him die as quickly and easily as possible. When the pain became overwhelming, he begged Garrett to kill him. "If you are a friend of mine, you'd put me out of my misery," he moaned. Garrett responded that they were hardly friends, particularly since the wounded man had tried to kill him "because I tried to do my duty."

The deputies had gone back to their poker game; one of them snorted, "Take your medicine." According to Garrett's account of the incident, O'Folliard replied, "It's the best medicine I ever took." Then Garrett said, "Your time is short." The dying man replied, "The sooner, the better."

He asked Kip McKinney, a posse member, to write a letter to his grandmother in Texas, telling her what had happened. Moments later, O'Folliard cried out, "Oh God! Is it possible that I must die?" Then, at Garrett's request, he named other members of the gang and where they were hiding. Jim East, one of the lawmen, gave him a cup of water. He drank some of it, shuddered, and died, forty-five minutes after he was shot.

He was buried the next day in Fort Sumner Cemetery. When the posse members went through his saddlebags, they found a letter he had written to his grandmother, telling her that he and Billy were planning to visit her in Texas.

Years later, Garrett described O'Folliard as "something of a gun expert, in his own belief at least. He was a man of medium height and dark complexion, and of no very great amount of mental capacity. He was one of those who wanted a reputation as a bad man."

However, Alexander McSween's widow, Susan, remembered him as "a good natured, rollicking boy, always singing and full of fun."

Four days after O'Folliard's death, on December 23, 1880, the remaining members of the gang were holed up at Stinking Springs. Relying on the information provided by O'Folliard and area rancher Manuel Brazil, Garrett and a large posse surrounded the crumbling rock house where the outlaws were hiding. In his book, *The Authentic Life of Billy the Kid*, Garrett described the situation:

> *I had a perfect description of the Kid's dress, especially his hat. I had told all the posse that, should the Kid make his appearance, it was my intention to kill him, and the rest would surrender. The Kid had sworn that he would never yield himself as a prisoner, but he would die fighting with a revolver at each ear, and I knew he would keep his word. I was in a position to command a view of the door-way, and I told my men that when I brought up my gun, to all raise and fire.*

So the lawmen hid and waited, once again braving near-intolerable frigid conditions, unable to start a fire because it would give them away. They waited a miserable four hours. One shivering posse member suffered from frostbitten feet; most of the others resorted to grumbling. Garrett toyed with the idea of sneaking into the house and getting the drop on the bandits who, unaware of what was waiting for them outside, slept and snored comfortably inside.

Finally, dawn came and the lawmen heard movement inside. A man appeared at the door, carrying a feed bag for the horses the outlaws were keeping inside. It was Charlie Bowdre, and he had no idea of the danger that awaited him. He resembled Billy, particularly in the early morning light, and he was wearing a sombrero similar to the one the Kid always wore, so Garrett raised his rifle and the lawmen began their assault. Bowdre was hit twice in the chest. The impact sent him reeling back inside the rock house, and his companions started returning fire while avoiding the hooves of their startled horses.

Minutes later, somebody inside the house yelled that Bowdre was dying and wanted to give himself up. Garrett shouted back that he should step outside with his hands raised. Suddenly, two shapes appeared at the opening where a door once hung. It was Billy, holding Bowdre's limp form in front of him. He shoved his friend through the doorway while hollering, "They have murdered you, Charlie! But you can get revenge. Kill some of the sons-of-bitches before you die!" Mortally wounded and unable to raise his hands, Bowdre staggered toward the posse, clutching his chest. He fell into Garrett's arms; the sheriff laid him on his own bedroll. His final words were, "I wish … I wish … I wish …," then a whispered, "I'm dying." He was thirty-two years old.

Aware that they were outnumbered and outgunned, Billy and the others surrendered. After taking the Kid and his cronies to a nearby ranch, where the rancher's wife fed them, Garrett sent a wagon back to Stinking Springs to retrieve Bowdre's corpse. The group then rode to Fort Sumner, where Bowdre's widow went into a murderous rage. She began cursing all the lawmen and then kicked and pounded on Garrett with her fists until she was pulled away. Still furious, she grabbed a branding iron and whacked the sheriff over the head.

To calm the grief-stricken woman, saying that he "held no grudge against the man," Garrett offered to buy a new suit of clothing for her husband's funeral, as well as pay for the grave diggers. Bowdre was buried next to O'Folliard in the former post cemetery at Old Fort Sumner. They had been shot and killed within four days and nineteen miles of each other. And Sheriff Pat Garrett had been instrumental in both deaths.

After Billy's death on July 14, 1881, his body was interred alongside those of his two saddle pals. But when the Pecos River flooded in 1889 and 1904, the waters swept away the original markers, making it almost impossible to identify the actual grave sites. However, old-timers who had once lived there were able to approximate the location by using remaining adobe walls and corners as reference points.

In 1931, Charles Foor, who had arrived in Fort Sumner shortly after Billy was killed, spearheaded a drive to create a suitable headstone for the three friends. It was cut from a thousand-pound piece of granite, inscribed with their names, the years of their births and deaths, and the word "Pals," and then placed at the site. The marker still denotes the triple grave, which is now surrounded by a wrought iron fence because thieves kept stealing the footstone that marked their final resting place.

CHAPTER FOUR
Bob Olinger:
Sweet Justice for a Killer Deputy

Bob Olinger was known for many things during his lifetime, most of them not very good. He worked both sides of the law and acquired a reputation as a cold-blooded gunslinger who killed with little or no provocation. But since his kind was common in the Old West, it took something even more notable to become a major footnote in history.

Olinger achieved such a niche, although not by his own choosing, when he became Billy the Kid's last victim.

And, although he was a lawman, there were no outbreaks of sympathy or calls for vengeance after Olinger's death. In fact, many who were there at the time not only felt he had it coming, but they even helped his assailant escape.

Olinger was not a well-liked person. He stood about six-foot-three, weighed about 240 pounds, was broad-shouldered, wore fancy clothing, carried a big knife, and walked with a swagger. He was also known as "Pecos Bob" and "Big Indian" and was considered the town bully in both Las Vegas and Santa Fe, where he used his knife-throwing skills to impress and intimidate the townspeople. He enjoyed getting into bar fights, playing poker, and threatening those who crossed him. More than once, those who disagreed with him wound up with mortal bullet wounds.

Born in Ohio in 1841, Olinger spent his formative years in Oklahoma and made his way to New Mexico in the early 1870s. He worked as a ranch hand and then was appointed marshal of Seven Rivers in 1876. The job didn't last long. He was fired because of his known association with rustlers, gamblers, and hard drinkers.

He stayed in Seven Rivers for a while, long enough to further his reputation as a killer. Three of his recorded victims made the mistake of challenging his honesty during poker games. The first was Juan Chavez, a cowboy who accused Olinger of cheating. Olinger stood up, hauled out his six-gun, and aimed it at Chavez, who was unarmed. When another player tossed his gun to Chavez, the two exchanged shots. Chavez missed; Olinger didn't. A bullet tore through Chavez's throat; he was dead before he hit the floor. Olinger holstered his gun, commented that "all's well that ends well," and casually walked out the saloon door.

John Hill was next. After losing all his money at the poker table, Hill loudly proclaimed that he had been set up, that Olinger had let him win a few small bets but then, when the stakes grew higher, so did Olinger's high cards. The poker-playing gunman laughed off the accusations, but when Hill left the saloon, Olinger allegedly shot and killed him.

Bob Jones also fell victim to Olinger's trigger finger. Like the others, Jones argued with Olinger after losing heavily in poker. But Jones was aware of what happened to Chavez and Hill, so he avoided a confrontation and left the saloon. Days later, Deputy Pierce Jones was ordered to serve a misdemeanor warrant on Jones and, although he had no capacity as a lawman, Olinger volunteered to ride along. Jones, the suspect, offered no resistance when the pair arrived at his home but did ask if he could tell his wife of his impending arrest. The deputy agreed; Bob Jones walked toward the house where his hunting rifle lay against a chair. Although Jones made no attempt to pick up the weapon, Olinger leapt at what he considered an opportunity to settle the grudge. He fired three times; all three bullets hit Jones in the back. Olinger brazenly claimed self-defense.

Deputy Jones charged Olinger with murder, and a trial date was set. But for reasons never revealed, the charge was dismissed and the case never came to court.

When the Lincoln County War broke out in February 1878, Olinger signed on with the faction headed by Lawrence Murphy and James Dolan, which opposed the group led by John Tunstall and Alex McSween over the control of dry goods merchandising in the area. The bloodshed eventually pitted ranchers, lawyers, merchants, and hired gunslingers against each other, and lasted for two years. Twenty-two men, including Tunstall and McSween, were killed in the fighting; another nine were wounded. Billy the Kid had allied himself with Tunstall, whose death set off a chain of events that would eventually result in Olinger's demise because, after learning of Tunstall's death, the Kid promised to kill everyone involved. Olinger was involved.

(Olinger's brother, John, also fought on the Murphy-Dolan side but settled down on a New Mexico ranch and lived a quiet life after the shooting was over.)

The Lincoln County War ended when Pat Garrett was named sheriff. The county supervisors also appointed his deputies, one of whom was Olinger. Garrett wasn't too pleased with the selection because he was aware of the new appointee's violent tendencies—something he would witness in person a short time later.

The two rode out of Lincoln to arrest an armed man. When they found him hiding in a ditch, Garrett promised that he would receive safe passage to jail if he surrendered without making any trouble. The fugitive threw down his gun and emerged from the ditch with his hands raised in the air. Olinger drew his six-gun, pointed it at the man's head, and threatened to kill him. In his version of the incident, Garrett said:

> When I brought out the man, Olinger came up on the run, with his cocked six-shooter in his hand. His long hair was flowing behind him as he ran, and I never in my life saw so devilish a look on any human being's face. He simply wanted to shoot that Mexican and he chased him around me until I had to tell him I would kill him if he didn't stop.

The episode ended when, for once, Olinger allowed common sense to overrule his quick temper, and he backed down. But it set the tone for what would be an uneasy relationship between the two during their relatively short period of service together.

The sheriff had earlier described Olinger as "a born murderer at heart" and said he suspected that Olinger "would have been glad to kill me for the notoriety of it. I never gave him a chance to shoot me in the back or when I was asleep."

He also explained how Olinger got the job despite his reputation: "Of course, you will understand that we had to use for deputies such material as we could get."

Aware that Billy the Kid would probably shoot him on sight if the two ever squared off, Olinger became obsessed with killing the young bandit. So when a reward was placed on Billy's head, Olinger viewed it as an opportunity to gun him down. But Garrett got to the Kid first, arresting him at Stinking Springs in December 1880. The Kid, along with comrades Dave Rudabaugh, Dave Pickett, and Billy Wilson, were returned to Santa Fe for trial. Wilson and Rudabaugh were remanded to other courts; the Kid was shipped down to Mesilla and tried for the murder of Sheriff William Brady. He was convicted and ordered back to Lincoln to be executed. Bob Olinger was part of the crew assigned to escort him between Santa Fe, Mesilla, and Lincoln.

And he hated his prisoner.

During the Lincoln County War, Bob Beckwith, a close friend of Olinger's, was killed, and Olinger blamed the Kid. That, coupled with his desire to make a name for himself by killing Billy, made the two bitter enemies who did little to conceal their hatred for each other.

On the train ride to Mesilla, Olinger sat next to the Kid, who was weighted down with heavy chains and constantly threatened by the shotgun and two pistols Olinger was wearing. The taunts were steady. Olinger reminded the Kid that "your days are short; I can see that rope around your neck now." Billy responded that events might not work out the way the killer deputy planned. Once the trial in Mesilla was over, Olinger won the bid to take him back to Lincoln. The presiding judge authorized a three-hundred-dollar payment for the successful completion of the job; the deputy chained his charge to the seat in a horse-drawn wagon, and the group set out for Lincoln. It's more than 140 miles from Mesilla to Lincoln, and Olinger, riding next to the Kid all the way, did his best to goad his prisoner into a fight, hoping that he'd do something rash and present an opportunity for the deputy to fulfill his obsession. He tormented young Billy constantly, poking, prodding, and jabbing him with his shotgun so often that even the other deputies displayed sympathy toward the Kid and distaste for their fellow lawman. But Billy resisted. At one point, he told Olinger, "Be careful, Bob. I'm not hung yet." Eventually, they all arrived safely in Lincoln. Olinger turned in an expense account of more than thirteen hundred dollars.

The execution was scheduled for May 13, 1881. Billy was placed in a room on the upper floor of the old Murphy and Dolan store, which was serving as the courthouse. The door had a lock, but it could be easily opened with a determined shove. Olinger was among the deputies assigned to guard him. The taunting continued. At one point, Olinger placed a loaded gun on a table where the Kid could easily reach it. Billy refused to take the bait. But the taunts never stopped, not even after Garrett warned Olinger to lay off.

The torment ended abruptly.

On April 27, about two weeks before the execution date, Garrett left Lincoln for a business meeting in White Oaks, about sixty miles to the west. He left Olinger and James Bell, another deputy, in charge of guarding the Kid. Toward noon, Olinger took five other prisoners to the Wortley Hotel, about a block down the road, for their lunch. Bell and the Kid remained behind, playing poker through the bars of the cell. What happened during the next few minutes remains a matter of historical speculation.

One way or another, the Kid got out of his makeshift cell, slipped out of his handcuffs, grabbed a pistol, and shot and killed Bell. One theory is that Billy asked to use the outdoor privy and Bell followed him outside, but let his prisoner get too far ahead of him on the way back to the second-story room where he was being held. The Kid got his hands free, raced up the stairs, got a gun, and fired at his captor. The first shot missed; the second was fatal. Bell ran down the stairs toward a corral but died after taking about fifteen steps. Another story suggests that a friend hid a gun inside the outhouse where Billy could find it. Under any circumstance, Bell was dead and Billy was free.

He grabbed Olinger's ten-gauge double-barrel shotgun and waited on the balcony.

Olinger was in the middle of his meal when he heard the two gunshots. He threw his flatware down, raced outside, and bumped into Godfrey Gauss, a German immigrant who was employed at the courthouse. A bewildered Gauss stammered out the news that Bell was dead and the Kid was loose and desperate. "He'll never get away from me!" Olinger cursed and ran toward the courthouse. He never got there. A few steps before reaching the front door, Olinger heard a familiar voice saying, "Hello, Bob." He looked up, directly into the barrel of his own shotgun. Billy didn't hesitate. A single blast sent Olinger to whatever fate would befall him after his death. He emptied the other barrel into the dead man's life-less form, broke the gun over the railing of the balcony, threw the pieces down at the lawman's body, and said, "Take it, damn you, you won't follow me anymore with that gun."

In his book, *The Authentic Life of Billy the Kid,* Garrett referred to the shotgun as "a very fine one, a breechloader" and wrote that Olinger had loaded it in front of the Kid, "putting eighteen buck-shot in each barrel." Garrett also quoted Olinger as bragging, "The man that gets one of those loads will feel it."

Gauss later told officials that he saw the tussle between Billy and Deputy Bell, then heard the initial shots and ran to the hotel where Olinger and the prisoners were eating. "I called to him to come quick," the eyewitness said. "He did so, leaving his prison-ers in front of the hotel. When he had come close up to me, and while standing not more than a yard apart ... he was struck by a well-directed shot ... and fell dead at my feet. I ran for my life to reach my room and safety, when Billy the Kid called to me, 'Don't run. I wouldn't hurt you. I am alone, and master not only of the courthouse, but also of the town, for I will allow nobody to come near us.' "

As the bodies of the two slain lawmen lay where they had fallen, Billy ordered Gauss to saddle up a horse and promised to leave town as soon as he got the shackles off his legs. Gauss said he gave Billy a small pick and the Kid worked for an hour, trying to remove the chains, but he couldn't get them all off. Nobody interfered, and he even chatted with some townspeople during the attempt. Finally deciding that he could remove the shackles somewhere else, he came down the stairs and said, when he passed Bell's corpse, "I'm sorry I had to kill him but couldn't help it." But when he reached Olinger's body, he nudged it with the toe of his boot and said, "You are not going to round me up again." Billy then shook hands with several onlookers, climbed into the saddle, and galloped away with the shackles still hanging from his leg.

Garrett recounted later that the town was so terrorized by the brazen escape and the two deaths that nobody extended any effort toward stopping the Kid. He noted that Billy "could have ridden up and down the plaza until dark without a shot having been fired at him, nor an attempt made to rescue him. A little sympathy might have actuated some of them but most of the people, doubtless, were paralyzed with fear."

The sheriff also blamed himself for what he called "a most distressing calamity" that came about due to carelessness and mismanagement on his part. He recalled, "I knew the desperate character of the man … that he was daring and unscrupulous and that he would sacrifice the lives of a hundred men who stood between him and liberty, when the gallows stared him in the face, with as little compunction as he would kill a coyote."

Billy's freedom was short-lived. Garrett ended it with a fatal shot three months later.

The bodies of Olinger and Bell were removed from the front of the courthouse and laid in a room until Garrett returned. A coroner's jury ruled that the two men had been killed in the line of duty and that "both came to their death by reason of gunshot wounds inflicted on them by William Bonney, alias Billy the Kid, while Bonney was held in custody for the murder of William Brady and was awaiting his execution upon the conviction of that crime and that [as] Olinger and Bell were guarding him they were murdered by said Bonney, alias Kid, in making his escape from custody."

Today, almost all of Lincoln is included in the Lincoln Historic District, which was declared a National Historic Landmark in 1960. Fourteen years later, the National Park Service said it was "the best preserved cow town in the United States."

Seventeen stone and adobe buildings, including the old courthouse, are owned by the state and operated as the Lincoln State Monument. The courthouse has been converted into a museum that features exhibits recounting the building's history as a general store, jail, residence, and Masonic lodge. Other buildings reflect the history of the town, which was originally called Las Placitas del Rio Bonito when founded in 1849. It was named Lincoln in 1869 and reached its peak population of eight hundred residents around 1880.

The Wortley Hotel, where Olinger never got to finish his last meal, is now a bed and breakfast on Highway 380 as it passes through Lincoln. The facility's advertising material mentions that guests "can eat with Bob Olinger and have your picture taken with him in the dining room with a collection of old maps, newspapers and paintings."

The property sits behind a white picket fence down the street from the old courthouse. Guests can relax on rocking chairs on the ninety-two-foot-wide front porch and sip an evening cocktail while viewing "the quiet beauty of the surrounding hills, mountain peaks and stars." The hotel no longer serves prisoners, but it does feature "real mashed potatoes." And the guests sleep on well-aged brass beds under the facility's motto: "No Guests Have Been Gunned Down in Over 100 Years."

Despite his rather notorious lifestyle and shady past, Olinger is still honored by the US Department of Justice. On Panel 13 of the National Law Enforcement Officers Memorial in Washington, D.C., he is listed as a lawman killed in the line of duty. The accompanying biographical data lists his age at time of death as forty, his rank as "deputy marshal," the cause of death as "gunfire," and the weapon used as "officer's shotgun." He was buried in an unknown grave at Fort Stanton Cemetery in Lincoln County.

But after his death, Olinger's own mother told a newspaper reporter, "Bob was a murderer from the cradle, and if there is a hell hereafter, then he is there."

Though long gone, Olinger lives on as a central figure in Billy the Kid movies. He has been portrayed by Leon Rippy in *Young Guns II* (1990), by R. G. Armstrong in *Pat Garrett and Billy the Kid* (1973), by Denver Pyle in *The Left-Handed Gun* (1958), by Alan Hale Jr. in *The Law vs. Billy the Kid* (1954), by John Merton in *I Shot Billy the Kid* (1950), and by Warner Richmond in *Billy the Kid* (1930).

CHAPTER FIVE

Whiskey Jim Greathouse:
Bad Companions Did Him In

Many outlaws in the history of New Mexico came to violent ends because they made poor choices when it came to selecting companions. Jim Greathouse was a prime example.

Not that he was a paragon of virtue himself. Hardly. He was a killer and a rustler who sold rotgut whiskey to Native Americans and bought stolen beef from cattle thieves. But he might have succeeded in legitimate business if he hadn't become associated with the likes of Billy the Kid and Joel Fowler.

Greathouse started his life of crime at an early age. Born around 1854 in Texas, he developed a shady reputation by age twenty. Lawmen in Texas regarded him as a notorious whiskey peddler who also took part in illegal buffalo hunts and raids on Indian hunting parties.

He tried to follow the straight and narrow a couple of times, but the path toward easy money was much wider and easier to traverse, so it always lured him back. By the time he arrived in New Mexico, he had already fought lawmen, the US Army, and Comanches. He also had acquired the nickname of "Whiskey Jim" because of his ability to drink voluminous amounts of alcohol. There are no actual records of how much he could pass down his gullet, but the folklore of the time said it was more than any other human could handle without falling down or passing out.

None of that did him any good when two bullets ripped through his upper body in the winter of 1881.

Seven years earlier, Greathouse was the object of an army campaign designed to get rid of him, one way or another. The troops were after him because he sold whiskey to the Indians, which led to uprisings, which usually led to deaths. Colonel Ronald Mackenzie issued the order to bring Greathouse in, regardless of whether he was breathing or not. The cavalry didn't catch him, but the threat was enough to force Whiskey Jim out of the whiskey business.

So he turned to cattle rustling.

Using the money earned from the sale of contraband whiskey, Greathouse formed a gang of thieves that raided north into Indian lands and west into New Mexico Territory. When they couldn't find any cattle to rustle, they stole horses and mules from buffalo hunters.

And he was crafty.

On more than one occasion, angry cattlemen and hunters stormed into the small Texas town that Greathouse was using as a headquarters, complaining about their pilfered livestock. Greathouse would listen intently and then make a gracious offer: He and his men would recover the stolen animals for a set amount per head. When the agreement was struck, the thieves rode out of town, went directly to where they had hidden the stock and, within a few days, triumphantly returned with the herd. The hunters and ranchers forked over the cash, unaware that their rescuers had stolen the critters in the first place.

The gang worked that form of extortion until the speediness of the recoveries became suspect and the victims began accusing him of stealing their animals, then returning them for a reward. Greathouse feigned righteous indignation, then cussed out his accusers and declared he would no longer deal with them. He left town almost immediately.

But trouble followed him, and this time it turned deadly. While still in Texas, two gang members stole horses from a freight outfit. They got caught, and the teamsters hanged them from the uplifted tongues of their wagons. Whiskey Jim heard about the incident and headed north, up to the Texas Panhandle, where he hooked up with a party of buffalo hunters. His new companions included Pat Garrett, Billy Wilson, Fred Kuch, and Jimmy Carlyle. All would become significant players in the rest of the Whiskey Jim drama.

During one of their forays, the group was attacked by a band of Comanches who resented the hunters' practice of killing the buf-

Whiskey Jim Greathouse rustled cattle and sold illegal liquor.

falo, stripping off the hides, and leaving the rest to rot or be eaten by varmints and buzzards. Garrett left in a hurry and headed toward New Mexico. Greathouse and the others fought off the attack, but fire destroyed their wagons and supplies.

While returning to safety, the survivors met José Tafoya, a trader illegally selling guns and ammunition to the Indians. After confiscating most of his merchandise, they shot and killed the man on the grounds that anyone providing firearms to the natives deserved to die.

Then they ran into another battle with the Comanches.

This time, they were surrounded by a group they figured was forty times larger than theirs. Even worse, a small band of Apaches had joined the Comanches. Greathouse was wounded but somehow managed to lead an escape by setting fire to the dry grass in which their attackers were sequestered. But that was enough Indian fighting for Whiskey Jim, so he headed west into New Mexico, eventually reaching Las Vegas.

He was right at home there because Las Vegas was the epitome of the lawless West. The town was filled with every known type of outlaw, saloons that never closed, brothels that welcomed business day and night, and gamblers who never knew when to quit and go home. Greathouse soon abandoned his careers in cattle rustling and extortion and became a full-time gambler. That didn't work out very well. Shortly after taking up the profession, he shot and killed four men in disputes over poker games. Although the law in Las Vegas was practically nonexistent, four killings were too much for even the lawless, so Greathouse was obliged to leave town—in a hurry.

In the summer of 1879, he bought a ranch along the Pecos River, not far from Anton Chico. But ranching didn't bring in money fast enough, so he resurrected one of the skills he had acquired and honed in Texas—he selected a partner and went back to cattle rustling. He kept some of the stolen cows to build his own herd; his partner sold the rest. And yet, although relatively successful, they weren't getting rich.

Then Fred Kuch, one of his buffalo-hunting cronies, reentered the scene. Things picked up rapidly, from a financial standpoint. Kuch had saved much of his earnings and agreed to go into the ranching business with Greathouse. They dealt strictly in cattle at first; within a year they were able to buy a larger ranch, then a store and roadhouse. A local newspaper noted that the Greathouse Tavern was "considerably better than any others in the area and customers are given a fair deal."

But the roadhouse was little more than a front. Greathouse and Kuch weren't running a legitimate business; they were operating a stopover for outlaws, affording them a place to hide until their pursuers gave up the chase. They were selective, however. Small-time crooks didn't get protection from the law because, Greathouse figured, they'd be easy to follow. Only the more notorious got shelter because they were smart enough to cover their tracks.

Over the next year, Greathouse was a suspect in the deaths of two mule skinners and a Las Vegas lawman. He was never charged in any of the murders, and it was business as usual at the tavern. That all changed when Whiskey Jim met Billy the Kid.

In November 1880, Greathouse bought a small group of horses and mules from the Kid, who was a regular guest at the roadhouse. Billy and his gang spent the money in saloons and brothels in nearby White Oaks and drew the ire of local lawmen after shooting out all the street lamps, a common practice among liquored-up men of the West. As they were leaving town, Constable T. B. Longworth organized a posse to bring them back. They followed the outlaws to the Greathouse Tavern, then surrounded the establishment and waited. It was the morning of November 27, and it was cold.

When Longworth decided to ride back to White Oaks to get reinforcements, he left deputies Will Hudgens and James Carlyle in charge. Soon afterward, the posse snared Joseph Steck, a freighter who had left the tavern to feed his horses. The frightened man said Billy and two members of his gang—Billy Wilson and Dave Rudabaugh—were inside, along with Greathouse, Kuch, and several other men. The lawmen sent the freighter back into the house with a note from Carlyle, demanding that the gang surrender. The demand was met with derisive laughter. The bandits were inside, they were warm, and they had food. They had no intention of surrendering to a shivering, hungry posse. They sent their own note back to Carlyle, rejecting his ultimatum. After two more written exchanges, Billy invited Carlyle inside so they could "talk this over like gentlemen and discuss the terms of surrender."

Carlyle refused but then agreed when Whiskey Jim stepped outside and offered himself as a hostage. The deputy unbuckled his gun and went inside while Greathouse settled down on the frosty ground with the posse members. Inside, Billy and Carlyle talked, but the discussion went nowhere so Rudabaugh and Wilson ordered the lawman to drink with them. Faced with six-guns pointing at his head, Carlyle took a drink, then another. By noon, all three were inebriated, and Carlyle was begging to be sent back to the posse. Meanwhile, Billy and the lawmen were still exchanging notes. As the standoff continued, Kuch replaced Steck as the note-bearer, darkness fell, and the situation grew even more tense.

Finally, the posse members could stand the cold no longer. It was near midnight, and they were tired of waiting. They sent Kuch back into the house with a note saying that if Carlyle was not returned to them within five minutes, they would kill Whiskey Jim.

Minutes passed. Both the chill and the tension were becoming unbearable. Longworth had not returned with reinforcements. Carlyle was now a prisoner, and the gang had forced Steck to fix them a meal. Nothing was going to be settled, and frostbite was becoming a potential problem for the posse.

Suddenly, there was a shot. A member of the posse, either by accident or on purpose, discharged his rifle. The lawmen feared the worst, and it happened.

When he heard the shot, Billy figured the posse had carried out the threat to kill Whiskey Jim. Worse than that, Carlyle apparently had the same thought so he made an escape attempt by throwing himself through a window. He got through the opening but never reached his companions. Within seconds, his bullet-riddled body lay still in the snow. With its leader dead, the posse released Whiskey Jim and withdrew, leaving Carlyle where he fell.

With the lawmen gone, the outlaws were able to ride away unimpeded. And nobody was certain who had killed Carlyle.

In a letter sent to Governor Lew Wallace, dated December 12, 1880, Billy claimed that after the initial shot was fired, "Carlyle thinking Greathouse was killed jumped through the window breaking the sash as he went and was killed by his own Party they think it was me trying to make my escape."

Wilson, while being held in Las Vegas later, supported the Kid's contention, saying that he didn't shoot at Carlyle and that he had tried to stop Billy and Rudabaugh from doing so. Rudabaugh allegedly called Wilson a "damned liar" and said all three had fired at the fleeing lawman.

The next day, another posse returned to the scene to retrieve the slain lawman's corpse. During the night, the outlaws fled back to their headquarters in Fort Sumner. Whiskey Jim and Kuch rode into Las Vegas. Two days later, a mob descended on the ranch and burned all the wooden buildings to the ground. Greathouse told the *Las Vegas Gazette* that the loss was "about five thousand dollars." He said he had no plans to rebuild.

He hung around Las Vegas until the spring of 1881, when he had an indirect encounter with another of his old buffalo hunting buddies, Pat Garrett.

Garrett had been appointed sheriff of Lincoln County with the expressed purpose of bringing Billy the Kid to justice. Greathouse heard about the situation and wrote to Billy, warning him to leave the territory. The letter was supposed to be delivered to a mail drop in Fort Sumner, but Garrett somehow intercepted it. That set into motion the series of events that led to Billy's demise.

Whiskey Jim kept a low profile until he was arrested in March 1881 and charged with being an accessory to Carlyle's murder. The charges were dropped, and Greathouse went back into business, this time as a freighter. He hauled across a wide area of the territory and, according to the *Las Vegas Gazette,* was "regarded as an honest man and any who have freight to be taken to White Oaks and elsewhere should make terms with him."

Once his business was well established and profitable, he turned it over to a manager.

And went back to stealing cattle.

He formed a new gang and stationed its members all over the territory. They rustled only a few head at a time to avoid suspicion and drove them to secret hiding places. Greathouse and other gang members then moved them for sale in local towns and mining camps. When another outfit tried to cut into his profits, Greathouse shot and killed one man and mortally wounded another. That took care of the competition.

Eventually, it was his cattle-rustling reputation that brought Whiskey Jim's career to an abrupt end. Curiously, however, he wasn't even involved in that particular theft.

Joel Fowler, who ran cattle in the Gallinas Mountains, had lost about forty head of steers to rustlers and tracked them to a ranch that Greathouse happened to be visiting. The rustlers, Jim Finley and Jim Kay, were also there when Fowler and his foreman, Jim Ike, showed up. Since Fowler had a nasty habit of shooting people from ambush, Finley and Kay drew their weapons and took a defensive stance. When Greathouse intervened, Fowler claimed he had just shot a man in Socorro and feared that the two men holding guns on him were out for revenge. Whiskey Jim's peacekeeping effort prevailed, and when things settled down, Fowler confessed that he knew about his savior's background and professed a great deal of admiration for him. The adulation, although probably false, worked like a charm, and they all rode out together, Fowler and Ike riding with Greathouse, Finley and Kay bringing up the rear.

When the unlikely quintet stopped for lunch, Fowler shot and killed Greathouse and Finley, and Ike gunned Kay down. Fowler claimed self-defense. He said Whiskey Jim drew first while shouting, "I know your game, Joel! It won't work with me!" But when lawmen from Socorro went out to get the bodies, they discovered that Greathouse had been shot twice, once in the back and once in the head. Nobody in New Mexico believed Fowler's version, but no charges were filed against him for the slaying.

After a lynch mob hanged Fowler in 1884, Ike told authorities that Fowler had stationed himself behind his horse and fired two shots at Greathouse as he was hoisting himself into the saddle. Greathouse, he said, had never removed his gun from its holster.

It didn't make any difference. Whiskey Jim Greathouse was dead and buried at age twenty-seven.

CHAPTER SIX

Bronco Bill Walters:
His Loot Is Still Buried

On June 16, 1921, an elderly man fell from a windmill while working on the Diamond A Ranch near Hachita, New Mexico. He suffered a broken neck and died about four hours later. His name was William E. Walters.

The death might have gone relatively unnoticed except for the irony involved.

And the unanswered question it left.

The irony was that years earlier, William Walters had faced death often, and had it occurred, it would have been the result of an act much more violent than falling off a windmill. And his demise on those occasions, had it happened, would not have been accidental. It would have been caused by a lawman's bullet or a hangman's noose because, in his prime, William Walters was among the worst of the bad.

He was known as Bronco Bill Walters, but he also went by Bill Anderson and Billy Brown. He was a killer and a robber whose exploits rivaled those of any of his contemporaries. He rode with Black Jack Ketchum, then formed his own gang and compiled an impressive list of murders, stagecoach holdups, and train robberies. He survived gun battles with lawmen, frequent jail time, and a seventeen-year prison term. He got away with hundreds of thousands of dollars in gold, silver, and cash but rarely spent any of it because, with the law always on his tail, he hid the loot and was never able to retrieve it.

So his death also raised the often-asked but never-answered question:

What happened to all that money?

Nobody knew then. Nobody knows today.

Bronco Bill Walters specialized in rustling cattle.
SCOTTSDALE CC SOUTHWEST STUDIES

There are few clues. On his deathbed, Walters asked to see a cowboy he had befriended while working as a wrangler on the ranch. The man didn't get there in time, but within hours the implied purpose of the former outlaw's death wish—that he was going to reveal where he had hidden the money—became a subject of intense speculation.

According to local legend, Walters had stashed his ill-gotten gains in several places, including caves and canyons in the nearby Sierra Ladrones (Robbers Mountain). Other stories claimed that most of it lay hidden under the dust and sagebrush near Solomonville, across the border in Arizona. And local folklore declared that Hachita residents had discovered caches of money, either while looking for treasure or stumbling over it by accident. Two fortune hunters from Albuquerque, prompted by stories that some of Walters's treasure was buried between two trees on a small hill east of the mountain range, spent months searching the area with Geiger counters. When they came across 332 silver dollars imprinted with dates between 1878 and 1898, they figured the rest had to be nearby. But they didn't find it.

The hunt grew particularly intense when José Jaramillo, a poor sheepherder, suddenly had enough money to build himself a fine house and acquire a large herd of sheep. The common theory around town was that Jaramillo had discovered the money shortly after an 1898 train robbery but was smart enough to keep it quiet until the furor died down.

Nobody looks for the lost Solomonville treasure any more—at least, not publicly. Things have changed substantially since Walters might have buried anything there. The town, named after German immigrant Isador Elkins Solomon, had its name shortened to Solomon in the early stages of the twentieth century and today has a population of about 250, down from the 1,300 who lived there during Walters's time. Now, one of its claims to fame is that Charles Stevens, a grandson of Geronimo, was born there. He later moved to Hollywood, became a well-known character actor, and appeared in more than two hundred movies, usually portraying a Native American or a Mexican.

Typical of characters from this era, the facts surrounding Bronco Bill's early life are as much a mystery as the location of his buried treasures. William Walters was definitely born at Fort Sill in Oklahoma Indian Territory, but there is disagreement about the actual year. Historians have recorded the date as either 1861 or 1869, with 1869 getting the most support. Like most other young men of that time period, his first job was herding cows. Next, he found work as a section hand for the Santa Fe Railroad and stayed with it until his late twenties. Then he figured out that robbing trains was much more lucrative than working for them. And so, he joined the already densely populated ranks of New Mexican outlaws.

He began riding with the Ketchum gang in 1893 but left within months, taking several Ketchum men with him to organize his own band of bandits. During his time with Ketchum, Walters was blamed for two shooting deaths. After branching out on his own, Walters concentrated on robbing Wells Fargo money carriers, specifically trains. He also was responsible for killing at least two more men, both of them wearing badges.

Before that, however, in October 1890, Walters and Mike McGinnis shot up the small town of Separ, between Deming and Lordsburg. They had planned to relieve a miner of his monthly income, but the intended victim escaped, along with his money. The two would-be robbers had already consumed ample amounts of Separ's best whiskey, so when their scheme fell through, they turned their anger on the town itself and began shooting aimlessly at local buildings. That spree ended when Sheriff Harvey Whitehill shoved a shotgun into Walters's face; both troublemakers surrendered. They were temporarily jailed in Lordsburg, then sent by train to Silver City, where they spent four months behind bars while waiting for a grand jury to go into session.

The lengthy jail stay ended on February 16, 1891, when the two got tired of jail food, overpowered a guard, took him hostage, and escaped. They released the guard a few miles outside of town. A posse formed but gave up the search after reaching the Gila River, the accepted border between Arizona and New Mexico. The two fugitives separated; Walters made his way into Mexico, but McGinnis was never heard from again.

US Deputy Marshal Cipriano Baca chased Walters to the Mexican border and then lured him back into New Mexico by inviting him to a dance in Columbus, just across the line. Once Walters set foot on American soil, Baca arrested him and hauled him back to Silver City to face trial. A jury found him guilty and sentenced him to a year in the penitentiary at Santa Fe. When he entered the prison on June 10, 1891, Walters reportedly was twenty-two years old; a local newspaper opined that a year behind bars "may change his determination" to become a bad man.

But he didn't stay for a full year. Given time off for good behavior, Walters was released after ten months. He found work on area ranches for a couple of years, then drifted back to Silver City and was arrested on a weapons charge. That cost him a two-month stay in jail. Then he was arrested on an armed robbery charge and taken to the county seat in Socorro. Once again, he spent his time looking at the outside world through a jailhouse window. But within days, Bronco Bill and nine others sneaked past a drowsy guard and escaped. This did not sit well with the citizenry, who complained that the prisoners were not guarded carefully enough and were given almost free run of the jail.

The escapees scattered. Some were arrested within days; Walters stole a horse and headed south. Authorities suspected that he had again fled to Mexico, but he was spotted in Deming, living with a woman. Lawmen surrounded her house and demanded that he surrender. Walters refused; a gunfight ensued. One deputy claimed one of his bullets hit the fugitive, but he escaped, crossed into Mexico again, and got involved in cattle rustling. After the thieves got the herd across the border, Walters took his share and went to El Paso—into the hands of authorities armed with a warrant for his arrest because he had stolen a horse the night of his escape from the Socorro jail. He was returned to Socorro, spent months in jail, was charged with theft, received a thirty-day sentence, and then was released.

His freedom was short-lived. A lawman from Silver City was waiting as he left his cell. He was returned to Silver City and accused of shooting at the lawmen who had surrounded him and his lady friend in Deming. This time, however, he was acquitted. But he wasn't safe from the long arm of the law.

Either unable or unwilling to stay out of trouble, Walters hooked up with the Ketchum gang, then broke away and allied himself with William "Kid" Johnson and Daniel "Red" Pipkin. From 1894 to 1898, the trio, along with incidental others, forcibly removed an undetermined amount of cash from Wells Fargo shipments. Several innocent men who tried to prevent the robberies became victims of deadly gunfire. None of this bothered Walters; he went right on stopping trains, blowing up safes, and running from sheriffs' posses.

After almost every robbery, instead of dividing up their spoils, Walters and his men buried the take in places they assumed they could easily find once they ditched the lawmen. Sometimes it was a matter of necessity because the loot was often in silver dollars, and saddlebags filled with silver dollars slowed down their horses. The heavy load made it easier for lawmen to follow their tracks and gain ground as they pursued the robbers.

But the authorities were relatively ineffective. Sheriffs had difficulty rounding up honest men to ride in a posse because many potential volunteers feared that the request to join the chase was a trick designed to sign them up for military service in the Spanish-American War—a common ruse at the time. So the robbery spree continued.

In the early morning hours of May 23, 1898, Walters and Kid Johnson waited in the darkness as southbound No. 21, a passenger train, arrived at the station in Belen. The two had ridden into Los Pueblitos, four miles to the south, the evening before. They stashed their horses there, walked into Belen, and hid in the shadows. The train stopped, the station crew loaded the mail and luggage, and the passengers boarded for the trip to Socorro, San Marcial, and on to El Paso. The locomotive belched and hissed, then lurched forward as the huge wheels began revolving. At that same moment, the two strangers leapt from their darkened hiding places and jumped onto the express car, always the first unit behind the engine.

They knew the routine and the exact timing it required, so they waited until the train was well away from the station. Then they scrambled over the coal tender unit, jumped into the engine cab, and shoved their six-shooters into the faces of the bewildered—and frightened—engineer and fireman. About a mile south of the station, they ordered the engineer to stop the train. Walters jumped out of the cab and, using the skills acquired during his days as a railroad worker, uncoupled the passenger cars. He got back into the cab and ordered the engineer to drive the remaining units—locomotive, coal tender, and express car—farther south before stopping again.

By this time, they were back in Los Pueblitos. The robbers rolled the safe out of the express car onto the ground, used dynamite to blast it open, and scooped out as much of the contents as they could carry. But before leaving the scene, they tossed a bag of money to the engineer and fireman. It was not a reward for their unwilling participation in the robbery; it was an apparent attempt to prove that they didn't harm anyone. It was a token gesture, based on the fact that the territorial legislature had, in 1897, passed a law demanding the death penalty for anyone convicted of assaulting a railroad passenger or employee while committing a robbery.

(The railroads had also tried a variety of measures to thwart the holdup men. One included the development of an alarm system that featured armed guards sitting in a glass case. It didn't work. Nothing worked. The editors of *Harper's Weekly* said as much by writing that the robberies might be prevented if the train passengers would rise up in armed protest against the bandits, but they then observed that none was brave enough for the task. The editorial concluded that all the safeguards "have been overcome by the natural cussedness of man.")

The take estimates from the May 23 robbery were never fully determined. Wells Fargo reported a loss of only $250; local legend said it was as much as $50,000. Either way, Bronco Bill and Kid Johnson rode off into the dark, heading southwest. They stopped to bury part of the money, then arrived in the village of Puertocito that afternoon. They bought food and moved on.

While the robbery was taking place, the train conductor and express guard raced on foot back into Belen to spread the word. But attempts to form a posse weren't met with much success, due to the fear of being recruited into the army. Additionally, Socorro County Sheriff Holm Bursum had to wait until Cipriano Baca, the deputy marshal, arrived from El Paso by train. But Bursum knew plenty about Walters; he had already locked him up on two occasions. The first time was for horse theft. Walters and nine others dug a hole in the jail wall and escaped. He stole another horse, got caught, and was returned to the pokey, where he stayed until January 1897. Within eight months, he robbed two more trains.

Once Baca arrived in Socorro, a four-man posse rode out after Walters and Johnson, determined to bring them in for the train holdup at Belen. Valencia County deputies Francisco Vigil and Daniel Bustamante agreed to go along on the chase. But Baca and Bursum ran their horses too hard and had to wait for fresh mounts to be sent from Socorro. Vigil and Bustamante went on alone. It was a fatal mistake.

The two Valencia County lawmen traced the robbers to the Alamo Indian community, where the deputies recruited some Navajo trackers to help them. One of the trackers found the outlaws' campsite; Vigil and Bustamante waited until sunrise to make their move. They took positions on a ridge overlooking the camp, then sent a tracker down to take the fugitives' horses from the tree where they were tied. When the sun crept over the ridge, Vigil stood up and yelled, "Raise your hands! I have warrants for your arrest!" But the demand was met with gunfire. Within seconds, Vigil and Bustamante were dead, and Johnson was wounded. Vicente Wuerro, the tracker, managed to fire two shots; both hit Walters. Although wounded, the outlaw was able to fire once. The Navajo also paid with his life.

And Bronco Bill escaped once more.

But Wells Fargo was fed up with these increasing reductions of its wealth. They hired Jeff Milton and George Scarborough, two of the toughest lawmen in the Southwest, to bring it to an end. The railroad donated a car to the operation, giving the badge-toters the ability to move quickly whenever they got a new lead.

The plan worked perfectly. Within two months, Milton and Scarborough tracked down Walters, Johnson, and Pipkin. During a gunfight along the Black River in Arizona, Walters and Johnson were wounded; Johnson didn't survive. Pipkin got away, but not before forcing the lawmen to retreat under a hail of gunfire. He raced to Johnson's body, removed his money belt, which allegedly contained as much as six thousand dollars, and escaped by crawling away through heavy gunfire.

US Marshal C. M. Foraker summarized the incident in his letter to the US attorney general: "It is with pleasure that I beg leave to report the arrest of Bronco Bill. Kid Johnson was killed. Bronco Bill was seriously wounded but I think he will come out alive under skillful medical treatment."

Bronco Bill did recover, but the gunshots had rendered his right arm useless. And his days as a murdering train robber were over. He was tried in 1899 on several charges, convicted on some of them, and sentenced to life in prison. However, he did have one more spurt of lawlessness when, on April 16, 1911, he escaped from the territorial prison at Santa Fe. The *Santa Fe New Mexican* reported the escape with typical frontier enthusiasm by reporting that the break was done "in a thoroughly thrilling manner worthy of the man and his career."

Kinch Mullins, a convicted murderer, also escaped but turned himself in the next day. Walters walked south along the railroad tracks, apparently headed for the Sierra Ladrones, where he had buried so much of his treasure. After breaking into a ranch house to steal some clothing, he got to Albuquerque unnoticed, spent the night there, then walked another fourteen miles to Isleta, where he was spotted by Charles Mainz, the Santa Fe Railroad's special agent. Mainz questioned him; Walters said he was a cattleman. But his lifeless arm gave him away. Mainz arrested the escaped convict and returned him to Santa Fe. His freedom had lasted three days before he was back in his prison cell, destined to serve out his term. Back then, however, a life sentence didn't actually mean imprisonment until death. Those drawing that penalty commonly served only about eight years. But the escape cost Walters, so he wasn't released until 1917. He went to Texas until his parole expired the next year, then returned to New Mexico and found work on a ranch.

Meanwhile, Pipkin made his way to Moab, Utah, where he became a sort of hero when he joined a posse and killed four rustlers. But the adulation didn't last. When Utah officials were informed that he was wanted in New Mexico, they arrested him and handed him over to a Wells Fargo agent, who hustled him back to New Mexico. Once confined, he faced a variety of charges, including train robbery and murder. He was freed on bond but was soon arrested by Arizona authorities and ordered to stand trial on a train robbery charge in the territorial court in Albuquerque. A jury found him guilty; he drew a ten-year sentence in Yuma (Arizona) Territorial Prison. He entered prison in October 1900 and, with time off for good behavior, was released in April 1907.

But his troubles weren't over. Oddly enough, his next confrontation occurred when he was on the other side of the law. In September 1918, while serving as a deputy in Gallup, New Mexico, Pipkin became involved in a dispute over the affections of a local woman, Dora Mattox. She resisted his advances, and during a public shouting match, Pipkin shot Pat Lucero, a town marshal who had intervened. That brought new charges; Pipkin was sent back to prison for two more years. After being released in 1920, he took a job as a watchman at a coal mine north of Gallup. Stricken with cancer, he shot and killed himself on July 6, 1938.

Years before, Walters had found work servicing and repairing windmills in the area around Hachita. On June 16, 1921, while standing atop a windmill platform on the Diamond A Ranch, he was knocked to the ground when the blades began turning. The fall broke his neck. Ranch hands carried him into Hachita. On his deathbed, he asked friends to contact another old cowboy from a nearby ranch. He said he wanted to tell him where the money was hidden. But he died before the man could reach him.

Wells Fargo never recovered any of its monetary losses, which were estimated at more than four hundred thousand dollars in the period between 1870 and 1898. One report put the total number of robberies during that stretch at 218. Seventy-eight people were killed, and another sixty-seven suffered gunshot wounds. Although Walters wasn't responsible for all those figures, he was credited with playing a major role in their compilation.

Despite that, Bronco Bill never got rich. He spent years searching but could not find any of the loot he had stashed. He looked for it in the mountain hideaways and scoured the low hills and sandy wastelands; his searches were always futile. Poor memory and the changing landscape were undoubtedly the primary reasons. There was also the possibility that someone else had found and removed his treasures. He never returned to Solomonville, giving rise to the theory that, in reality, he had never hidden anything there. Or maybe, as some suppose, he was simply tired of it all and wanted to become plain old William E. Walters, a ranch hand.

But in the hills that surround Sierra Ladrones, the legend persists that Navajo fathers still pass down silver dollars to their sons.

CHAPTER SEVEN

Shady Ladies:
Adultery Was Almost as Popular as Rustling in the Old West

Although most of them weren't actually criminals, women of questionable repute played a major role in the history of New Mexico. Some were prostitutes, some were wayward wives, and some were outlaws, as mean and ornery as their male counterparts. Many of them outlived one or more husbands and usually prospered with each passing.

Bronco Sue Raper was like that. She either married or lived with at least four men, and they usually came to unfortunate ends.

She was born in 1844, either in England or Australia, but her family immigrated to Nevada when she was a teenager. Her parents worked in the mining camps, where the miners took her under their wings in a frontier version of guardianship, teaching her how to ride a horse and shoot a rifle. When she was fifteen years old, her family moved to California. Within a year, Sue Warfield became Sue Raper, following her marriage to Tom Raper, a transplant from Indiana. They had a son, Joseph, and moved to Nevada, where she bore two more sons, Robert and William.

The marriage didn't last long. Tom Raper was seriously wounded during an Indian attack in 1865; the injury crippled him, and it wasn't long before Sue got tired of taking care of him. She packed up the kids and left, then hooked up with a former US Army officer. That relationship didn't fulfill her needs, either, so she became a cattle rustler and jewelry thief around Carlin, Nevada. And she was good at it, soon earning the nickname "Bronco Sue" and a reputation for being the most notorious rustler in the state.

Accused of grand larceny for her steer-stealing and gem-heisting operations, she left Nevada and moved to Pueblo, Colorado, using the alias of Susan Stone. Months later, she relocated to Alamosa, Colorado, where she invested her ill-gotten gains in a stage line that ran between San Antonio and Conejos. By 1882, however, she had sold out and arrived in Española with Jake Younker, her new husband. They opened a saloon in the area, then moved to White Oaks, where Younker died of smallpox. Bronco Sue dug a grave, buried him, and moved in with Robert Black without the sanction of a wedding ceremony.

The new couple relocated to Socorro. She ran a boardinghouse; he opened a saloon. But they had a falling-out over money. Black got drunk and made threats; she had him arrested and promised to shoot him if he didn't leave her alone. He didn't leave her alone. Their relationship came to a fiery end on August 6, 1884, when she fulfilled her promise with a slug from a revolver. A grand jury heard her plea of self-defense and found her not guilty.

Then it was on to Doña Ana County for the multi-widowed Bronco Sue. She met and married Charles Dawson, who would live to regret the union, but not for very long. Dawson suspected his new bride of having an affair with John Good. During a bitter fight over range rights, Good shot and killed Dawson in a face-off on the streets of La Luz, a small cow town near Tularosa. Bronco Sue, aware of the trouble brewing between the two, had armed herself with a rifle and followed her husband because he was accompanied by his stepson, William, Bronco Sue's youngest child. She said later the rifle was to protect her son, not her husband.

Good was arrested and pleaded self-defense. Bronco Sue testified against him, but to no avail. He was acquitted. But then she was arrested on a charge of killing Robert Black, her previous paramour. During the ensuing trial, her son William testified that she had killed Black to prevent him from telling the authorities about her days as a cattle rustler. Despite that, she was acquitted and soon disappeared from the annals of history.

But her legend stayed behind. In a way.

Her nickname closely matched that of a more renowned outlaw, Bronco Bill Walters. And her son was named William. That led to an assumption that Bronco Sue Raper's son William was actually Bronco Bill Walters, the notorious outlaw. Although the claim had no basis in fact, it gained credibility when a US commissioner for the First Judicial District of New Mexico issued a warrant "to apprehend Bill Raper, alias Bronco Billl." Bill Raper had been charged with assault with intent to kill, but the case was dismissed after a hearing. The same hearing revealed that Bill Raper could not possibly be Bronco Bill due to dissimilarities in dates, locations, and physical features of the two.

Susan McSween earned a niche in New Mexico's history for a couple of reasons.

First, she was married to Alexander McSween, one of the principal characters in the Lincoln County War. His death at the hands of the rival Murphy-Dolan gang is listed as the final act of the war. Second, she apparently was not a faithful wife.

During and after the five-day shoot-out that cost her husband his life, Susan had a bitter confrontation with Colonel Nathan Dudley, commander of an army unit involved in the dispute. In retaliation, Colonel Dudley dug up some dirt on her by procuring affidavits from Lincoln County residents who knew Mrs. McSween. He said he did it to protect himself against court actions she was threatening against him.

His findings indicated that Susan McSween was "a lewd woman without principle." One statement said that she had no respect for her "marriage obligations" and that she frequently violated them. Another said that she had worked in a brothel before marrying McSween and that she was a woman of "loose character."

Sheriff George Peppin, an employee of the Murphy-Dolan outfit, told Dudley that Susan was "bad, unprincipled, lewd and untruthful" and that he had seen her in "actual lascivious contact with a well-known citizen." He continued that he had also watched as she engaged in "lascivious contact" with another man and said it was "too disgusting to relate."

The most damning testimony came from Francisco Gomez, a twenty-one-year-old laborer who told Dudley that he initially believed Mrs. McSween to be a respectable woman until she began making improper advances toward him. Those advances, Gomez said, soon led to sexual intercourse, "committed at various places, chiefly in the brush near the river."

Susan McSween withstood all the allegations and accusations, however. After her husband's death, she became wealthy through the settlement of the estates of men she believed were responsible for what she considered murder. Although others also filed claims, she got all the money and wasn't willing to share. In the words of one associate, "Mrs. McSween is not going to pay any creditors except herself."

Ada Hulmes boldly strode into the pages of New Mexico's criminal history books on February 19, 1889, when she shot and killed her former lover in Silver City.

She and her victim, John V. Brown, had been carrying on for quite some time, even though he was married and the father of two children. But the passion cooled and on that fateful night, he sent her a note saying he wanted to end the affair. He sent another note at the same time to Ada's roommate, Claude Lewis, asking if she wanted to become his mistress.

Furious, Ada Hulmes grabbed a pistol, stuck it down the front of her blouse, and said she was going to the saloon where she worked as a piano player and where he dallied as an unfaithful husband. Once there, she said, she was "going to kill the son-of-a-bitch." Although Ada knew about the second note, she asked her roommate to go along. Claude Lewis declined at first because she didn't want to get involved in any trouble. But Ada assured her that she would not cause any problems, so they headed for the bar.

Once there, Ada marched into the crowded back room where Brown was watching a card game. She withdrew the pistol and loudly announced her intentions. Brown reacted instantly, dashing behind a stove that separated him from the irate woman. It didn't do him any good. She fired one shot; it tore through the stove and into his cowering body. He stumbled out of the room and fell dead on the sidewalk in front. Ada fled out a back door and ran into Savannah Randall, who worked as a laundress during the day and as a lady of the evening after sundown. Randall hid her in one of the cribs behind the saloon, but sheriff's deputies soon arrived, kicked in the door, and arrested Ada.

She came out screaming, flailing her arms, and "yelling like a hyena." She protested her innocence and then pretended to be insane. Her trial began in Las Cruces in October 1889. Her slim defense rested on the premises that she had been insane with jealousy, that she did not remember anything from the time she read the note until she was taken to jail, and that she had shot Brown in self-defense. A doctor testified that she suffered a "loss of accountability." Her attorney went into great detail about her early life, when her father died unexpectedly and her mother went insane. He noted that she had married young but to an abusive husband who abandoned her and their daughter and that she was forced to take up playing the piano in saloons to support herself.

The prosecution didn't take up much time, merely noting that Ada Hulmes had "committed a dastardly and unprovoked murder." The jury retired. Some wanted the death penalty; others held out for prison sentences, one as short as three weeks. Eventually, they found her guilty and recommended a three-year term behind bars. She entered the territorial prison in Santa Fe on October 30, 1889.

Apparently, incarceration wasn't so bad. The *Albuquerque Daily Citizen* asserted that she enjoyed comforts and privileges not available to other convicts, that her cell was a "large, airy apartment on the third floor," and that she had a carpeted floor, a piano, and a sixty-dollar-a-month matron tending to her needs. The *Las Vegas Optic* joined the fun, alleging that an ex-prisoner had given a reporter inside information that two prison employees were enjoying sexual favors from Hulmes. Other newspapers jumped on the story. The *Albuquerque Morning Democrat* proclaimed that "there is a skeleton in the penitentiary closet [and] every attempt is being made to hush up the matter."

In the meantime, Hulmes began campaigning for her release. She claimed that prison life was ruining her health and asked

Governor L. Bradford Prince to visit and discuss her physical and mental conditions and her request. He declined. She wrote again, claiming that she needed a pardon or commutation so she could "secure her child's future." She contacted New Mexico's solicitor general, who took her side, saying that she should never have been convicted and that she had been "cruelly abused by the public and the press."

But Mary Teats, head of the Women's Christian Temperance Union, supported the courts, contending that Hulmes was dangerous and "a contamination [who] wished to go back to her former wicked life."

Doctors soon joined the fray as Hulmes supporters. One wrote that continued imprisonment threatened both her mental health and physical health. The prison physician callously observed that "[Ada] is a nymphomaniac, and to such an extent does she practice this vile habit, that she has developed a suicidal mania. If she is not released from the Penitentiary … she will soon be a raving maniac with no hope of ultimate recovery." Another physician wrote, "We have enough insane people in our Territory without deliberately making another."

Then a man claiming to be her long-absent husband, Edward Sheehan, showed up on June 2, 1891, and talked with authorities. He told them that Ada could straighten herself out if she were released and allowed to reunite with her child in Chicago. This time, the officials listened. Governor Prince granted her a full pardon on June 29, 1891.

That night, according to a report in the *Santa Fe Sun,* Sheehan got drunk while Ada and a convicted horse thief "made a night of it at the dance halls and brothels."

When the editors of the *Optic* heard of her release after serving less than two years, they were furious. They opined: "The career of this woman, and the connection of some of the territorial officials therewith, is one of the most remarkable and shameful pages in all the history of New Mexico. It is doubtful that its equal can be found in the civilized world."

Almost a year later, a Silver City newspaper reported that she was appearing in a variety show in Creede, Colorado. That was the last mention of Ada Hulmes.

CHAPTER EIGHT

John Joshua Webb:
Another Lawman Gone Bad

The early residents of Las Vegas showed very little respect for the sanctity of their town's original name. Way back in the early 1600s, the first settlers called it Nuestra Señora de los Dolores de Las Vegas Grandes (Our Lady of the Sorrows of the Great Meadows). The later, and more permanent, settlement was established by a Spanish land grant in 1835 as part of Mexico and became a part of the United States following the Mexican-American War. Once the new alignment was in place, the city drew pioneers, settlers, and merchants in large enough numbers to make it one of the few notable towns along the Santa Fe Trail as it wound its way across the emerging territory.

But the prosperity attracted another element—the bad guys.

And the bad guys would sully any religious intent expressed by those who gave the town its first name.

By the mid-1870s, half of Las Vegas was controlled by a corrupt gang of thieves, robbers, murderers, and bunko artists who had migrated from Dodge City, Kansas. Once established, they gained power through political appointments, latching on to such prime jobs as justice of the peace, city marshal, and chief of police. Using those positions as fronts, they rustled, killed, and robbed at will, throwing fear into the hearts of honest citizens with a type of vigilante law based on the Old West rule of "shoot first, then ask questions." They ruled the east half of the city. The west half, across the Gallinas River, was home to honest working people, most of them of Mexican descent.

Around 1876, the city erected a windmill in the town plaza. But things were so bad that it soon became a vigilante gallows where criminals and suspected lawbreakers were sent dangling to their dooms, whether convicted or not.

J. J. Webb was jailed and shackled after a lengthy career as an outlaw.
LAS VEGAS CITIZENS COMMITTEE FOR HISTORIC PRESERVATION

So Las Vegas was already a well-established den of iniquity when John Joshua Webb rode into town. He had spent considerable time in Dodge City, and he was no stranger to violence because, while there, he had worked both sides of the law. Sometimes, he worked both sides at the same time.

Webb soon discovered that Las Vegas had a familiar feel to it. A multitude of saloons supplied whiskey and women to the soldiers at nearby Fort Union, the railroad workers laying the tracks for the Atchison, Topeka and Santa Fe line, and the long list of nefarious characters passing through to somewhere else. Most of them arrived on one of the six trains that stopped in Las Vegas every day, and they included the infamous—John Henry "Doc" Holliday, Wyatt Earp, Jesse James, and Billy the Kid—and the lesser knowns, who went by such names as Rattlesnake Sam, Cockeyed Frank, Web-Fingered Billy, Hook Nose Jim, and Handsome Harry.

John Joshua Webb fit right in, as both a peacekeeper and an outlaw.

He was born in 1847 in Keokuk County, Iowa, but his family left Iowa and settled in Nebraska in 1862, when John was a stripling of fifteen years. In 1871, at age twenty-four, he traveled west and spent much of his adult life as a lawman. But he also worked as a teamster, buffalo hunter, surveyor and, occasionally, as a hired gun. He readily found employment in these trades across Nebraska, Kansas, Colorado, Wyoming, and South Dakota.

After moving to Kansas, he served as a deputy under Ford County Sheriff Charlie Bassett and his top assistant, Bat Masterson, in Dodge City. He rode with the posse that unsuccessfully pursued Sam Bass and his gang after they robbed a Union Pacific train of sixty thousand dollars. When Masterson became sheriff, he deputized Webb again, this time to go after six outlaws who had held up a train at Kinsley, Kansas. Two gang members were captured within days; one of them was Dave "Dirty Dave" Rudabaugh, who would later become a Webb ally in New Mexico. Rudabaugh initially resisted arrest, but Webb drew first and forced him to surrender. The other four accomplices were apprehended later. Five members of the gang drew prison sentences, but Rudabaugh testified against them and promised to go straight, so he was released. He headed for New Mexico. He didn't go straight.

The bandits weren't the only threats, perceived or otherwise. While trying to live a peaceable life as a businessman, Webb was called back into action in September 1876, when Chief Dull Knife and his Cheyenne tribe escaped from an Oklahoma reservation. Most of the troops from Fort Dodge set out in pursuit, which left Dodge City vulnerable. The alarmed citizens, frightened by rumors of impending massacres, sent urgent messages to state officials that they needed men and guns. They received some weapons, but fewer than twenty soldiers were still on duty at the fort. So the fort commander selected Webb and two others to go on scouting missions to see how many Cheyennes were out there. Their report only heightened the tension. They told authorities that about two hundred Indians were in the area and that they weren't looking very friendly.

Instantly, rumors of death and destruction raced through the area, and the local newspapers fueled the frenzy with headlines declaring, in essence, that "not a woman or child in Nebraska or Kansas is safe." The panic subsided only after it became clear that Dull Knife and his followers meant no harm; they only wanted to return to their ancestral homelands in the Black Hills of South Dakota.

Tired of the unsettling conditions in Kansas, Webb moved to Colorado and again tried to settle down and become a businessman. But his reputation followed him. By 1879, he was working as a hired gun for the Atchison, Topeka and Santa Fe railroad in a battle with the Denver and Rio Grande line over right-of-way allotments through the Royal Gorge. When that dispute ended, Webb moved again, this time to Las Vegas, where his life and lifestyle would undergo drastic changes. The man who was respected as a leading citizen and sometime lawman in Kansas and Colorado met some of his former cronies in the wide-open town and, after a brief time, he joined them on the path that led directly to crime and punishment.

The change wasn't immediate. Shortly after his arrival, Webb and Holliday formed a business arrangement and bought a saloon. This was an ideal situation for Holliday because he was already a notorious and quick-tempered gambler, so he worked the tables while Webb tried to keep the peace and tended to the finances. They were both playing poker on the night of July 19, 1879, when they became involved in the incident that would lead to the dissolution of their partnership. As they sat dealing, raising, and betting, Mike Gordon entered their establishment and began yelling obscenities and creating a general disturbance. Gordon, an ex-soldier widely regarded as a bully, loudly demanded that one of the saloon girls, the one he called his girlfriend, accompany him as he left town. The young woman denied any relationship with the loudmouth, so Webb ordered Gordon to leave the premises. He did, but not before more cursing and a warning that he would return and forcibly take the woman with him.

Holliday followed the man outside. Within seconds, two gunshots shattered the uneasy calm. Gordon fired first, but he missed. Holliday, always calm, got off the second shot. He didn't miss. Gordon died the next day. Two days later, the word around town was that Holliday was about to be arrested and charged with murder. He immediately surrendered his share of the saloon's ownership to Webb, hustled out of town, and headed back to Dodge City, where he hoped to rejoin Wyatt Earp. But Earp had left for Tombstone, so Holliday followed him. A little more than two years later, they became principal characters in western gunfighter lore due to their involvement in the shoot-out at the OK Corral on October 26, 1881.

Webb operated the saloon alone until 1880, when he was named city marshal. Soon after, he joined the Dodge City Gang, so named because many of its members had been associates in Dodge City, where they served as lawmen, hit men, or just plain criminals. At the time, it seemed like an obvious choice since Webb knew many of the gang members from his time in Dodge City. It was not, however, his wisest decision.

His former associates had acquired respectable positions as lawmen and jurists, but they were actually stealing cattle, money, and anything else they could lay their hands upon. Hyman "Hoodoo Brown" Neill, the gang leader, was justice of the peace; Dave Rudabaugh, Webb's onetime enemy, was a police officer. Other outlaws and gunfighters were assigned to lesser positions. For more than two years, they thumbed their noses at the laws they were supposed to be enforcing while establishing a reign of terror. They held up stagecoaches and trains; they rustled cattle; they were involved in multiple murders and lynchings.

It was a perfect setup. While others committed the actual crimes, Webb and other badge-wearers helped cover their tracks and provide them with alibis. The city's vile reputation spread. As historian Ralph Emerson Twitchell observed later, "Without exception, there was no town which harbored a more disreputable gang of desperadoes and outlaws than did Las Vegas."

Neill had a particularly interesting background. After serving in the Union army during the Civil War, he settled in Missouri and worked for a print shop. But one day, after being sent out on an errand, he hopped a freight train and headed west. He worked as a gambler and a con man, then went to Mexico with a friend and started an opera company. When that didn't make him as rich as he expected, he drew the final curtain and moved to Las Vegas. By the time he got there, the town was already recognized as one of the worst places in the territory. Neill, now better known by his nickname "Hoodoo Brown," found all that to his liking, so he set up shop. He ran for mayor and was elected. Later, he appointed himself coroner, then justice of the peace. In that latter position, he organized the gang and announced that it would serve as the city's police force. And as coroner, he could readily dismiss any fatal gunshot wound as either justified or a matter of self-defense.

In January 1880, Joe Carson, a gang member and the town's US marshal, was shot dead in a brawl. He had gone to a saloon, owned by one of his fellow outlaws, and tried to corral four rowdies who were shooting up the town and creating a general disturbance. Las Vegas had adopted antigun laws that required everyone to surrender their weapons when entering a business place. When Carson ordered them to obey the law, a gunfight broke out. Carson fell to the saloon floor, mortally wounded; his deputies killed two of the assailants. Webb and six others later surrounded a house where the two remaining killers were hiding and ordered them out. They surrendered after the posse assured them of a fair trial. It didn't happen. After Webb placed them in jail, a mob broke in and took them to the windmill on the plaza for an unauthorized execution. But they were spared hanging when Carson's widow arrived on the scene carrying a rifle. She shot and killed both men before the vigilantes got their ropes strung.

Webb's time with the gang was brief. His downfall started on March 2, 1880, when he shot and killed Mike Kelliher, a freighter. Around 4 a.m., Kelliher and some friends had stopped at a local saloon for liquid refreshment, but they refused to give up their guns when Webb and other bogus lawmen ordered them to put their pistols on the bar. "I won't be disarmed," Kelliher retorted. "Anything goes." He reached for his gun but never got it out of the holster. Webb drew and fired. He got off three shots. Two hit Kelliher in the chest; the other smashed into his head.

A coroner's inquest noted that the dead man had been carrying a large amount of money and it was missing. That may have been a determining factor when Webb, regardless of his position as city marshal, was tried and convicted of murder. Sentenced to death by hanging, he was tossed in the same jail he had once guarded.

There was speculation that Neill had taken the money and fled town because, by this time, the townspeople had had enough. Tired of the continual escapades, they posted a notice in the *Las Vegas Optic* under the heading: "To Murderers, Confidence Men, Thieves." It read:

The citizens of Las Vegas have tired of robbery, murder, and other crimes that have made this town a byword of every civilized community. They have resolved to put a stop to crime, if in attaining that end they have to forget the law and resort to a speedier justice than it will afford. All such characters are therefore, hereby noticed that they must either leave this town or conform themselves to the requirements of law, or they will be summarily dealt with. The flow of blood must and shall be stopped in this community, and the good citizens of both the old and new towns have determined to stop it, if they have to hang by the strong arm of force every violator of the law in this country.

It was signed: "Vigilantes."

But the lawlessness didn't stop. Not right away, at least. While Webb sat in his cell awaiting execution, Dave Rudabaugh unexpectedly broke into the jail in an attempt to free him. Rudabaugh shot and killed a jail guard, but the jailbreak wasn't successful. Webb remained incarcerated while his would-be rescuer fled, only to be arrested later that year. Webb's death sentence was commuted to life imprisonment, and he and Rudabaugh were both sent to prison.

They mounted two escape attempts during their time there. On September 19, 1881, they acquired guns and, along with two other prisoners, tried to shoot their way out. It was not successful; one would-be escapee died during the gun battle. But they were determined, and this determination led to success when, in late November 1881, Webb, Rudabaugh, and five others chipped a seven-by-nineteen-inch hole through a cell wall, squeezed through, and got away. The two former comrades-in-crime fled to Texas, then Mexico, where Rudabaugh was ambushed and killed outside a cantina in a remote town named Hidalgo de Parral. Legend says that he was decapitated and the villagers paraded his head around town.

After leaving Las Vegas, Neill moved to Houston, Texas, where he was arrested and jailed on charges from Las Vegas. While he was behind bars, Joe Carson's widow, Elizabeth, visited him, and the two began (or continued) a romantic affair. A local newspaper reported that the meeting was "said to have been affecting in the extreme, and rather more affectionate than would be expected under the circumstances."

Another paper's story was even more direct: "The offense committed at Las Vegas, as near as we can gather the facts relating to it, was murder and robbery, and the circumstances connected with the arrest here would indicate that the lesser crime of seduction and adultery was connected to it."

Neill was eventually released when Texas authorities were unable to pin anything on him. Then, according to a report in the *Chicago Times,* he and the widow were seen "skylarking through some of the interior towns of Kansas ever since." He ditched his female companion and went to Mexico, where he was allegedly killed during a gambling dispute.

J. J. Webb eventually grew tired of his life as a fugitive in Mexico and returned to Kansas, where he adopted the alias of "Samuel King" and worked as a teamster. Later, he moved to Winslow, Arkansas, and worked on the railroad. He died of smallpox there in 1882.

But his story didn't quite end there. In 2007, Engel Auction Company of Ennis, Montana, offered to sell a collection of Old West jewelry. One item was a gold pocket watch inscribed: "To my partner and friend John Joshua Webb, July 4, 1879, in Las Vegas N.M. John H. Holliday."

The timepiece sold for $41,650.

With the departure of the outlaws/lawmen, things settled down. Today, Las Vegas shows little evidence that it was once a town divided by crime. Situated as it has been since its inception in the foothills of the Sangre de Cristo Mountains, it is, according to a tourist brochure, "a small, vibrant city on the edge of rolling green-gold prairie, a city whose land speaks of the fire-roasted chile and reflected sun. The scent of juniper and piñon welcomes you to a tree-lined city that ranchers, artists and families who have lived here for hundreds of years call home."

And today, it is known primarily for a couple of interesting things:

First, although it traces its beginnings back to 1835, it is frequently accused of taking its name from Las Vegas, the gamblers' Mecca in Nevada. But the locals are quick to point out that "that other Las Vegas," as they call it here, wasn't established until 1905.

Second, it is a prime destination for architecture buffs and city planners. Most of the city's architectural heritage centers on a group of stone residences, commercial buildings, churches, and schools. Many of them are still standing in excellent condition after more than a century of use, sturdily constructed when the arrival of the Atchison, Topeka and Santa Fe Railroad ushered in wealth and better building materials to replace the traditional adobe blocks.

The newly rich lured stonecutters and masons to Las Vegas and employed their talents to build ornate houses in the Victorian, Queen Anne, Romanesque, Italian Villa, and Folk Renaissance Revival styles. Many of them were built using sandstone quarried along the railroad tracks about four miles south of the city.

The city gained national attention in 1912 when Jack Johnson, the country's first African-American heavyweight champion, successfully defended his title against Jim Flynn there.

The plaza that was once the site of the infamous hanging windmill is now a quiet park, filled with a bandstand and mature trees, and surrounded by some of the stately old structures. Las Vegas now boasts more than nine hundred buildings on the National Register of Historic Places. Curiously, one of them is the former home of Vicente Silva, the leader of merciless gangs that terrorized the city and surrounding area in the 1890s. Today, it is referred to as "a fascinating house [that] could be called a New Mexican folk style, Renaissance Revival residence. The elegant Palladian windows and alternating bands of red and tan sandstone are a surprise here or anywhere. Many people believe this was the home, headquarters or den of iniquity for the lawless gangs of local outlaw Vicente Silva."

Las Vegas is popular in other areas. The big screen, for example.

Moviemakers first took notice of the city around 1913, and Tom Mix, hero of the silent westerns, spent much of his time there while filming black-and-white shoot-'em-ups. Jack Nicholson came to town in 1969 to film portions of *Easy Rider*. Las Vegas was renamed Calumet, Colorado, when the 1984 film *Red Dawn* was shot there. Parts of the 1994 movie *Speechless,* starring Geena Davis and Michael Keaton, were filmed there; so was John Travolta's *Wild Hogs* in 2007. Also in 2007, the Coen brothers, Joel and Ethan, selected Las Vegas as the setting for their award-winning film *No Country for Old Men*. The 2009 thriller *Not Forgotten* was shot in Las Vegas, as were portions of *Due Date,* a 2010 production starring Robert Downey Jr. and Zach Galifianakis.

The city is home to New Mexico Highlands University and Luna Community College, while the United World College sits atop a hill in nearby Montezuma. And the fifteen thousand or so who live there also note, with considerable pride, that the last remaining Andrew Carnegie–sponsored library in New Mexico is in their town.

So today, John Joshua Webb would hardly recognize his old stompin' grounds.

Except some of those old buildings might look a bit familiar.

CHAPTER NINE

The Unrecognized Worst of the Worst:
Not All the Bad Men Gained Historical Notoriety

While most of the criminally focused attention in New Mexico's early history was directed toward the likes of Billy the Kid and Clay Allison, several others of their kind went about their lawbreaking ways with substantially less public notice. They included the usual assortment of bad guys, but their deeds of dishonor never attracted the frontier media. In other words, they didn't get enough publicity, so their claims to fame slipped quietly into the pages of history as mere footnotes.

One of them was David "Davy" Crockett, who sullied the name of his famous ancestor by committing a series of crimes in the 1870s. He was the nephew of Davy Crockett, the hero of the Alamo, but his lifestyle was drastically different. Born in Tennessee, he moved to Texas and was imprisoned for some unknown crime. He escaped and wound up in Cimarron, New Mexico, where he worked on a ranch and repeatedly expressed a deep-seated hatred of blacks.

Crockett spent much of his spare time in area bars and gambling halls and soon established himself as a bully. On the night of March 24, 1876, while drinking with Gus Heffron, his foreman at the ranch, he had a confrontation with Private George Small, a member of the US Ninth Cavalry, the black unit also known as the Buffalo Soldiers. According to witnesses, Crockett shot and killed Small, then turned and fired at three other members of the unit who were playing cards in the saloon. Two of them—Private Anthony Harvey and Private John Hanson—died. Crockett and

Heffron fled from the scene on foot because their horses were in the same stable as the soldiers' mounts.

After being captured, Crockett declared that former slaves should not be allowed to wear army uniforms because it was insulting to white troopers. He appeared before a Cimarron justice of the peace, who acquitted him of murder on the grounds that he was drunk at the time but fined him sixty dollars and court costs for carrying a gun.

The not-guilty verdict emboldened Crockett and Heffron. In the months that followed, they became belligerent nuisances who frequently rode their horses into saloons and, at gunpoint, forced patrons to buy them drinks. Then they'd shoot holes in the ceiling of the bar. Eventually, the townsfolk got fed up with this behavior, so the local sheriff and two deputies armed themselves with double-barreled shotguns and rode to the ranch to arrest the pair. As they waited near the barn, Crockett and Heffron rode up and were ordered to surrender.

Crockett merely laughed at their command and jokingly told them to shoot. They did; Crockett was mortally wounded. The blasts startled the suspects' horses, and they galloped away with the lawmen in pursuit. Crockett's horse finally stopped near the Cimarron River. The sheriff had to pry Crockett's hands loose from a death grip on the saddle horn. Heffron got away but was arrested a short time later. He escaped from jail and fled to Colorado.

The Stockton brothers were born and raised in Texas, then migrated to New Mexico around 1874. They all came to violent ends.

Isaac "Ike" Stockton ran a saloon in Lincoln, then moved to Colfax County and became involved in the Colfax County War. He and his brother, William Porter "Port" Stockton, then moved to Trinidad, Colorado Territory, but after Port killed a man there, they relocated to the western part of New Mexico. They posed as cattlemen but were actually running a band of robbers known as the Stockton Gang that operated along the Colorado–New Mexico border.

The brothers got involved in a bitter feud with area cattlemen who accused the Stocktons of rustling their steers. Accusations and denials flew, and gunfire and lynchings followed. In August 1881, Burt Wilkinson, a member of the Stockton Gang, shot and killed a Colorado lawman and a twenty-five-hundred-dollar reward was posted for his arrest. Ike Stockton turned him in, claimed the reward, and felt no guilt when the nineteen-year-old Wilkinson was lynched.

Port Stockton allegedly began his life of crime when, at the age of twelve, he killed a man in Texas. After moving to Cimarron, he shot and killed another man but was acquitted of murder on the grounds that it was self-defense. Port and Ike then moved to Trinidad, where Port killed another man in a saloon brawl. He was jailed, but Ike helped him escape. Shortly afterward, he was again charged with murder, this time for the death of a man in Otero, New Mexico. He escaped from jail again and reappeared in Colorado, where he was twice appointed marshal of small communities. But he was fired from both appointments when the citizens uncovered his shady past.

Port's undoing was the result of crashing a Christmas party at a ranch near Farmington. He and three friends rode into the gathering uninvited, and one of the guests, along with one of the party crashers, died when a gunfight broke out. Days later, area ranchers posted thousand-dollar rewards for the trio, and on January 4, 1881, Sheriff Alf Graves and an eighteen-man posse went to Stockton's ranch to make an arrest. Stockton answered a demand to surrender by opening fire on the lawmen. They returned his fire, and Stockton fell dead.

Ike Stockton vowed revenge. But he had to be careful because Colorado authorities had dug up an old warrant issued against him for the murder of a man in New Mexico. Despite that, he rode into Durango the following September. Somebody recognized him and notified the law. A gun battle followed, and a bullet shattered Ike's knee. In an effort to save him, the town doctor amputated Ike's leg, but he didn't survive the surgery and died on September 27, 1881.

Sam Stockton, the third brother, used the name "West Brown" when he and an accomplice showed up at a Las Vegas ranch try-

The ghost town of Shakespeare was once the scene of a double hanging.

SAM LOWE PHOTO

ing to sell a string of horses they had illegally obtained in Texas. But before the transaction could be completed, Stockton was shot by John Farrington, the range boss at the ranch that owned the horses. The two rustlers tried to get away but were apprehended and jailed in Las Vegas and then sent back to Texas, where Sam was wanted for killing a Texas Ranger.

He escaped and fled to Colorado, but his freedom was brief. In April 1880, vigilantes hanged him for a murder committed during a robbery.

Obviously, vigilante hangings were almost common during those years. Two more notable incidents occurred about the same time in Shakespeare, one of the freewheeling communities that had sprung up in the late 1800s.

Shakespeare is a ghost town now, but once it was a mining boomtown with a population of more than three thousand and a rough reputation. It had twenty-three saloons, but not a single church, school, or newspaper. About the only law was an unwritten rule that if you shot someone, you had to bury him. Since the ground in and around the community was primarily rock, the rule held the murder rate down. This made it an ideal hangout for the likes of Sandy King and William "Russian Bill" Tattenbaum.

King was associated with the Clanton Gang in Tombstone in eastern Arizona Territory, and he took part in several armed robberies and cattle rustling operations. He also became friends with Tattenbaum during that time. When the tensions between the Clanton faction and a group led by Wyatt Earp reached a dangerous level, King left Tombstone and settled in Shakespeare; Tattenbaum followed. The two supported themselves by stealing cattle.

King had acquired a reputation as a hard-drinking gunman who was often the instigator of barroom brawls. As a result, he was also known as the town bully. He got away with most of his misdeeds until he got into an argument with a storekeeper, shot the man's finger off, and was hauled off to jail.

Tattenbaum, on the other hand, was a colorful character, best known for his seemingly outrageous claims that he was the son of a wealthy Russian countess. His dress was immaculate, his hair and mustache were always carefully preened, and he carried expensive pistols. But he was also a cattle rustler. He was out plying that trade when King was arrested, but he got caught and was thrown in jail alongside his partner.

Justice was swift in Shakespeare. Although there was no official court system, a hastily organized vigilante committee met in the dining room of the Grant Hotel and found Tattenbaum guilty of rustling. He was sentenced to death by hanging. Then a committee member recommended that King undergo the same fate, on the grounds that he was "a damned nuisance." The committee agreed. The two were dragged from jail to the hotel dining room, which had been selected as the execution site because there were no trees in town big enough to serve the deadly purpose.

As the lynch mob crafted the nooses, Tattenbaum begged for his life. King made a brief statement, saying that others had committed worse crimes but were allowed to escape death. He cited the case of Beanbelly Smith, who shot and killed Ross Woods in a quarrel over who was going to get the last egg at breakfast. Their pleas fell on deaf ears. The nooses were placed around their necks, and the ropes were thrown over the ceiling beams. The mob pulled the two up off the floor, and they were left hanging, even after they were pronounced dead.

The bodies were still there the next morning when the stage arrived and the passengers entered the dining room for breakfast.

Joel Fowler was another victim of an impromptu hanging. And by most accounts, he probably had it coming.

In 1883, Fowler stabbed James Cale, a traveling salesman, during a drinking bout in Socorro. Cale became annoyed when Fowler began shooting at an elderly man's feet to make him "dance." When Fowler laid his six-gun on the bar, Cale told the bartender to hide it. Fowler overheard the request and became angry. When the barman refused to return his gun, Fowler pulled a knife and stabbed Cale, who died three days later.

Fowler was arrested and charged with murder. It wasn't the first time. While he sat awaiting trial, another warrant was issued, this one for the murder of two ranch hands, Poney Diehl and William "Butcher Knife" Childs. Diehl was the brother of a man Fowler had killed a year earlier, after Fowler accused him and two others of rustling his cattle. At that time, killing a rustler was considered a legitimate act, so Fowler never came to trial.

Once he discovered the family relationship, Fowler had paid the surviving brother off and they parted company. But Diehl and Childs planned to ambush and kill Fowler at a place called the Stone House. Childs was killed in the gun battle that followed Fowler's arrival at the house, and Diehl ran inside the building. When the owner of the property arrived, he ordered Diehl out of the house and kicked the door in. Diehl shot and killed him, then again refused to come out. The next morning, Fowler ordered his men to set fire to the house. As it burned, they heard a single shot. When they were able to search through the ashes, they found Diehl's body.

Fowler was confident that he'd be found innocent, so he turned himself in, gave his side of the story, and was tried and acquitted the next day. But public opinion was building against him. Rumors emerged that his cattle herds grew larger while the herds of others became smaller. And that he'd sometimes sell his cattle, then steal them back. His background was catching up with him.

He allegedly killed a man he caught in bed with his wife. In May 1880, he shot and killed two drunks in Las Vegas. He considered it his civic duty; he was never charged with a crime. After the Diehl brothers and Childs were slain, however, the citizens of Socorro formed the Committee of Safety to combat crime under their own rules. Fowler was brought to trial for the death of James Cale.

His jury was composed of twelve Hispanics, none of whom spoke English. His defense attorneys argued that since he was drunk when he inflicted the fatal wound, he should be charged with a lesser offense, something like murder four, which carried a sentence of less than seven years and a five-hundred-dollar fine.

The judge used formal courtroom language to explain this to the jurors, none of whom understood a word he was saying. Despite that, or perhaps because of that, the jury found Fowler guilty of first-degree murder. His attorneys appealed. Fowler's date of execution came and went. The *Las Vegas Optic* editorialized that Fowler might not get the punishment he deserved. The Committee of Safety held a special meeting.

On January 22, 1884, a crowd of about two hundred masked men dragged Fowler from his jail cell and escorted him to a large cottonwood tree. While some of the vigilantes fashioned a noose and tied the rope to a tree limb, others held Fowler upright and off the dusty street. When the rope was placed around his neck, the men let him fall. But the rope stretched so much that his feet touched the ground. His executioners tried to retie the knot, but it was too tight. Determined to carry out their intent, five vigilantes grabbed Fowler's body and hung on it until he died of strangulation.

For days afterward, curiosity seekers and townspeople cut off pieces of the tree and took them home as souvenirs. A neighbor finally chopped the tree down to get rid of the crowds.

Dave Mather was another notorious character who worked on both sides of the law during New Mexico's territorial days. He spent his youth in Connecticut and even signed on as a sailor during his teens. But that didn't last long; he jumped ship after a year and headed west. Once across the Mississippi, he began a life of crime, some of it while wearing a badge. He reportedly was run out of Mobeetie, Texas, for trying to sell fake gold bricks. His alleged accomplice was Wyatt Earp. Later, he joined a group of gunslingers recruited by Marshal Bat Masterson to help settle a dispute between two railroads in Dodge City, Kansas. Because he was a loner who never talked about his past, he was tagged as "Mysterious Dave."

He arrived in Las Vegas, New Mexico, in the summer of 1879 and allied himself with the nefarious Dodge City Gang a short time later. The gang, composed of former Dodge City lawmen, controlled almost every criminal activity in the community, so it was probably not surprising that within a month of his arrival, Mather was charged with aiding and abetting a train robbery. The case was dismissed when nobody showed up to prosecute him. US Marshal Joe Carson then hired him as a deputy. In one of his first acts as a lawman, Mather arrested several military men for disorderly conduct. He wounded one of the soldiers and was taken to task by the local newspaper for being too aggressive.

Four cowboys killed Marshal Carson in a local saloon in January 1880 after he demanded they surrender their weapons. Mather, acting as his deputy, drew and fired, killing one assailant and wounding another so badly that he died a short time later. The other two escaped but were caught two weeks later and thrown into a Las Vegas jail. During the interim, Mather went about his duties as a deputy marshal. Three days after Carson's death, he shot and killed a drunken telegraph operator. It was ruled justifiable homicide and that, combined with his actions during the saloon shoot-out, drew high praise from the citizenry.

Two weeks after Carson's death, Mather got word that the other two gunmen were hiding on a nearby ranch. He organized a posse, found them, and returned them to Las Vegas. A masked lynch mob broke into the jail and hauled the prisoners to the town square for an illegal execution. The word around town was that Mather was a member of the mob, but nothing was ever proven. And the lynchings never took place because Carson's widow showed up with a rifle and killed both men before they could be strung up.

Mather's term as a Las Vegas lawman ended when he was forced to arrest two fellow deputies—J. J. Webb and Dutchy Goodlet—on a murder charge. He turned in his badge and left Las Vegas, headed for nowhere in particular. Eventually, he wound up back in Dodge City, where he served as an assistant town marshal and then owned a saloon. He shot and killed a rival saloon keeper and was involved in the death of a gambler. He was arrested, then released on three-thousand-dollars' bail but skipped town before legal proceedings started.

His final years were never recorded. There were rumors that he was spotted working on the railroad while living in the Nebraska wilderness. Another story had him moving to Vancouver, British Columbia, where he served with the Royal Canadian Mounted Police. The most widely accepted version, however, is that he was shot and killed in Dallas, Texas, in 1886.

Years later, western author Louis L'Amour summed up Mather's personality in his book, *The Empty Land.* He wrote: "Dave Mathers didn't wait for you. If you came to town talkin' loud about what you intended to do, Dave would find you and shoot you before you even got started."

John Kinney, a native of Massachusetts, came to New Mexico after being mustered out of the US Army in 1873 at the rank of sergeant. It didn't take him long to decide which side of the law he preferred. First, he took up rustling. Then he organized a gang of about thirty rustlers who were also responsible for several murders and property thefts. Soon, the John Kinney Gang was recognized as the most feared band of outlaws in the territory.

Territorial law was weak, so the outlaws ran things on their own terms until New Year's Eve 1875. While celebrating in the saloons of Las Cruces, where the gang usually stayed when not out stealing cattle, Kinney and three gang members—Jesse Evans, Jim McDaniels, and Poney Diehl—got into a brawl with a group of soldiers stationed at nearby Fort Selden. The outlaws didn't fare well against the military—the soldiers pummeled them to the floor and then unceremoniously tossed them out into the street.

Hours later, however, the quartet of bad guys returned to the saloon. But they didn't go back in. Instead, they stood out in front and opened fire. When the shooting stopped, two soldiers and one civilian were dead and three others were wounded. The gunmen fled and were never arrested for that particular crime, so they continued their deadly march along the criminal path. Jesse Evans left Kinney's gang and formed his own outfit, but the groups continued to collaborate in a variety of illegal enterprises. They were both hired by the Dolan-Murphy faction during the Lincoln County War, and they also participated in "the chain gang," a sort of marketing process in which one gang would rustle cattle and sell them to another gang, which would sell them to another gang. The exchanges continued until the stolen cattle were moved to market with no record of the original owner or the original thief.

Before his involvement in the Lincoln County conflict, Kinney had killed Ysabel Barela on the streets of Mesilla, just south of Las Cruces. He and several gang members fled to Silver City and went right on rustling until they were hired to fight in another skirmish, this one in Texas. In June 1878, they went to work for the Dolan-Murphy combine. During that conflict, Kinney boasted that he had already killed seventeen men, including Barela. The law finally came down on him when, on November 30, 1878, he was arrested and charged with Barela's murder.

It didn't matter. He was acquitted, and he and his gang returned to their outlaw ways. But then, Kinney switched sides. He worked as a scout for the army and later as one of the deputies assigned to escort Billy the Kid from Mesilla to Lincoln after the Kid was found guilty of murdering Sheriff William Brady and sentenced to hang.

Kinney's past caught up with him, however. He was arrested in 1883, charged with cattle rustling, found guilty, fined five hundred dollars, and sentenced to a five-year term in the federal prison at Leavenworth, Kansas. He paid the fine and served three years. By the time he was released, most of his old associates were either dead or in prison, so Kinney went straight.

He moved to Kingman, Arizona, and operated a cattle feed lot for a while. When the Spanish-American War broke out, he enlisted and served in Cuba. When that fracas ended, he returned to Arizona and became a successful miner, digging into the hills almost until his death in 1919.

CHAPTER TEN

Milton Yarberry:
A Lawman Who Went to the Gallows

Milton Yarberry's life paralleled the lives of many of his contemporaries. He worked both sides of the law, killed a few men, and always claimed the killings were done in self-defense.

And in the end, he met the same fate as many of his contemporaries: a violent death.

He was able to convince juries of his innocence several times. He had friends in high places and powerful enemies. But when it came time for final judgment, frontier justice and his enemies prevailed.

His path to the gallows began around 1849, when he was born in Walnut Ridge, Arkansas. It ended on a February afternoon in 1883, when he told a hangman in Albuquerque that he was executing an innocent man.

In between those dates, Milton Yarberry had a multilayered career. He was a cattle rustler, saloon keeper, murderer, brothel owner, hired gun, Texas Ranger, robber, posse rider, and lawman. Strangely, he escaped prosecution for most of his unlawful acts but was sentenced to death for shooting a man while wearing a badge.

The victim was Charles Campbell. He died on June 18, 1881. Yarberry was the prime suspect. The incident unfolded as Yarberry and Frank Boyd sat in front of a mutual friend's house in Albuquerque. They were an unlikely pair because Yarberry was the town marshal and Boyd was a well-known gambler. As they sat discussing the events of the time, they heard shots emanating from the direction of a nearby restaurant. Both ran toward the restaurant; Yarberry stopped to ask a bystander to identify the shooter. The informant pointed to a man walking away from the scene.

There were contradictory accounts of what happened next. Yarberry claimed he was acting in his official capacity when he

Milton Yarberry paid the price for being a gunslinging lawman.

ordered Campbell to stop so he could question him. Within seconds, the man was dead from gunshot wounds, including one in his back. Yarberry and Boyd were arrested.

During the preliminary hearing to determine whether either, or both, should be bound over to face trial on a murder charge, Yarberry insisted that Campbell was probably drunk at the time because he had a reputation for over-imbibing and because he became hostile when he drank too much. So when Yarberry ordered him to halt, Campbell drew a gun and turned toward the lawman. That, Yarberry testified, left him no choice. He had to shoot. Twice. Boyd said he also fired twice. Prosecutors pointed out that one of the wounds was in Campbell's back; Yarberry said it must have happened when his first bullet hit the man with such force that it spun him around.

Their testimony was convincing; both men were cleared. But the public didn't like the decision. Pressure grew, and Yarberry was arrested again on the same charge. When he realized that he would probably face the same fate, Boyd fled to Arizona. His freedom was short-lived. Within a year, he was slain by Navajos who hunted him down after he killed a member of their tribe.

On May 11, 1882, a grand jury indicted Yarberry on a murder charge. Legislators and authorities alike were tired of the lawlessness that had been the ruling force in the territory. They saw the trial of Milton Yarberry as an opportunity to set an example. The prosecution was vigorous, headed by New Mexico Attorney General William Breedon. He found Thomas Parks, a Nebraska attorney, to testify against the defendant. Parks had not testified at the preliminary hearing, but now he was a star witness. He told the jury that he had observed the shooting and, even more damaging to Yarberry, he swore he had seen the marshal shoot Campbell in the back. Even worse for the defense, Parks claimed he never saw a gun in Campbell's hand.

Yarberry's attorneys argued that Campbell had been armed and that his gun had been fired at least once. When put on the witness stand in his own defense, Yarberry stuck to his story that he shot Campbell because Campbell tried to shoot him. But Parks also refused to alter his testimony, and the jury apparently put more truth in his version than anything offered by the defense. The trial lasted three days. The verdict was "guilty." The sentence was "death by hanging." The execution date was set for June 16, 1883, to allow time for appeals. Yarberry was jailed in Santa Fe because sentiment against him was so high in Albuquerque that law officials feared a lynching attempt if he was kept there.

The time in jail probably gave him an opportunity to think about what had transpired in his relatively young life. It had been interesting, to say the least.

His name, according to later research, was not Milton Yarberry; it was John Armstrong. His life as a criminal began around 1870, when he was involved in the killing of a man in a land dispute in Sharp County, Arkansas. He fled from the scene. In 1873, he took another step toward his eventual destiny when he killed a man in Helena, Arkansas. This time, he left the area and hooked up with outlaws Dave Rudabaugh and Dave Mather. The trio staged several robberies in Arkansas and Missouri and were accused of murdering a wealthy rancher. Faced with arrest in Arkansas, they rode into Texas and split up.

A short time later, Yarberry (or Armstrong) apparently changed his name to John Johnson and settled in Texarkana, Arkansas—but not for long. In 1875, he shot and killed a man because he thought the victim was a bounty hunter out to take him, dead or alive, and collect the two-hundred-dollar reward offered in connection with the Sharp County killing. He didn't wait around for a coroner's jury to make a decision. He returned to Texas and became a Ranger. Although his personnel records indicated he was a good Ranger, he stayed with the unit for less than a year before moving to Decatur, Texas.

But his troubles kept finding him.

While in Decatur, he formed a business partnership and opened a saloon. But one day in the summer of 1876, another bounty hunter showed up and started asking questions, specifically about the Sharp County killing. His bullet-riddled body was found days later outside Decatur. No charges were filed, but the suspicions and accusations were pointed directly at Yarberry (or Johnson), and they grew stronger when he sold his share of the saloon to his partner and hurried out of town.

His next stop was Dodge City, Kansas, but he didn't stay long before heading for Cañon City, Colorado, where he went back into the saloon business, this time under the name of Milton Yarberry. His partner was Tony Preston, who would inadvertently become a key figure in a later Yarberry escapade. Apparently business was not very good, as illustrated in a story told by Eddie Foy Sr., the well-known country entertainer. In his memoirs, Foy wrote that he and his acting partner, Jim Thompson, were hired to perform in Yarberry's establishment, but when they finished the engagement, they were told there wasn't enough money to settle the account. Unable to collect, Thompson stole a barrel of whiskey, a rather brazen act considering Yarberry's reputation as a gunslinger.

Later, between 1910 and 1913, Foy and seven of his children formed a family vaudeville act known as "Eddie Foy and the Seven Little Foys." The group toured the nation for more than a decade and appeared in a motion picture. They were also the subjects of two later movies.

Yarberry did take gun in hand in March 1879 when a bartender at the saloon shot Preston. Yarberry fired three shots at the assailant but missed; he then joined the posse that captured the man. Preston recovered, but Yarberry had had enough of Cañon City so he sold his share of the saloon and left town.

Brothel owner became the next entry on Yarberry's résumé. After leaving Cañon City, he moved to Las Vegas, New Mexico, and opened a house of joy that catered to railroad workers. He also kept his six-gun in working order. He was a suspect in the robbery and murder of a freight hauler but avoided charges. In late 1879, he killed a man in a local hotel, allegedly after a fight over a prostitute. Again, he escaped prosecution on the grounds that it was self-defense.

However, that episode convinced Yarberry that his time in Las Vegas had come to an end, so he sold his share of the brothel, moved to San Marcial, New Mexico, and became reacquainted with Tony Preston, his former partner.

He also became reacquainted with Tony's wife, Sadie.

When he left San Marcial within months, Sadie Preston and her four-year-old daughter went along. Apparently, Milt and Sadie had been carrying on for a while, going back to their time in Cañon City.

The trio eventually moved to Albuquerque, where Milton became friends with Perfecto Armijo, the sheriff of Bernalillo County. The friendship proved beneficial for Yarberry because Armijo used his influence to land him the job as Albuquerque's first town marshal. It was an ideal situation for Yarberry: He was allowed to carry a gun and shoot people, all in the name of justice. It didn't take long for him to put that principle into effect. Weeks after becoming a lawman, Yarberry shot and killed two men. He got away with the first shooting, but the second one was his undoing.

In early 1881, Harry Brown sauntered in Albuquerque, talking loud and bragging that he was the son of a former Tennessee governor and that he had once helped derail a robbery attempt by Dave Rudabaugh in Kansas. He claimed he had killed several men but could never remember any specifics when questioned. He also drank heavily, which led to rumors that he was ill-tempered and quick on the draw. Despite all that, Sadie Preston became attracted to the newcomer, and the attraction developed into a romance. This did not bode well for Brown.

On the night of March 27, 1881, Sadie arranged a meeting with her new lover at a local restaurant. And she talked Yarberry into baby-sitting her daughter. But as the two were dining, Yarberry came marching down the street, heading toward the restaurant and holding the little girl by the hand. In an apparent attempt to avoid trouble, Brown stepped outside the eatery, but Yarberry strode right past him and handed the child over to her mother. When he came back outside, the two men began arguing as they walked to a nearby vacant lot. Once there, Brown punched

Yarberry in the face and drew his pistol. He got off one shot that hit Yarberry in the hand. Yarberry reacted instantly. Before Brown could fire again, the lawman drew his own gun and fired twice. Both shots hit Brown in the chest. He died on the spot.

Yarberry was arrested by his friend, the sheriff, and a preliminary hearing was held within days. Witnesses friendly to the defendant testified that Brown had openly and frequently announced that he intended to kill Yarberry and that Brown had fired first. Once again, Yarberry claimed self-defense. "Brown used some of the vilest language he could lay his tongue to," he told the jury. "He was, I could see, trying to get the drop on me." He continued that after Brown drew his gun and fired the shot that inflicted a "trifling scratch" on his thumb, "I realized that I must either kill him or die, and quicker than it takes to tell, I whipped out my gun and began firing."

Once again, he was cleared. But the decision was met with a major outcry from prominent Albuquerque citizens, who demanded a grand jury indictment. The body met in May 1881; after defense attorneys presented several witnesses to retell their stories, the result was the same. Yarberry was released and went back to work as the town marshal.

But less than a month later, he shot and killed Charles Campbell and his fortunes turned bad. Real bad. Death by hanging bad.

When the testimony and the final arguments were over, the jury met for only ten minutes before returning the guilty verdict. A cell in the Santa Fe jail waited for him.

But only temporarily.

His appeals were being denied as quickly as they were being filed. Yarberry realized that the eventuality of certain death was near; he had nothing to lose, so he decided to make a break for it. On September 9, 1882, he and three others filed through their iron leg bands, overpowered a guard, and escaped. One man was recaptured within hours; Yarberry and the other two got out of town before a posse chased them down. Santa Fe chief of police Frank Chavez apprehended Yarberry about twenty-eight miles from the jail. More appeals followed. So did more denials. As the inevitable drew closer, Yarberry fell into a deep depression, convinced that the whole world was against him. He tried to find relief with alcohol, drinking at least a bottle of whiskey every day. He told his keepers that he would break down without the liquid antidepressant. The constant drinking began taking its toll. He lost weight, and his normally ruddy complexion paled. When a reporter asked about his condition, he replied, "I ain't sick, and I ain't scared, either."

He was returned to Albuquerque to await the hangman's noose. It was nothing new in New Mexico, and it would continue after Yarberry's execution. From 1848 to 1912, territorial courts ordered more than one hundred death row criminals to undergo a similar fate, but only forty-nine of them were actually hanged. All but one were convicted of first-degree murder. The lone exception was Tom "Black Jack" Ketchum, who was executed for "assault on a railway train." Some were spared when their sentences were commuted to life imprisonment; some were given gubernatorial pardons; some escaped from jail.

And, despite what movies depict and folklore maintains, almost none of the legal executions during that time period used a tree as the key element. Lynch mobs used trees, telegraph poles, even store signs. But legal hangings were carried out on a specifically constructed gallows or scaffold. Yarberry's instrument of death was elaborate and relatively new. Most of the condemned died when a trapdoor beneath their feet was sprung open and they plunged to their death. But Yarberry was to be killed by a system designed to jerk the victim upward when the rope holding a heavy weight was cut. Although the results were the same, this method was praised as "the latest model of scientific skill" and was supposedly based on drawings found in a science magazine.

As he sat in his Albuquerque jail cell, Yarberry told a friend that his name was not Yarberry or Johnson. He said it was John Armstrong. He had changed it to protect his family's good name. On his last day, he asked for a priest so he could be baptized as a Catholic. Then he put on the new suit Sheriff Armijo had bought him, ate his final meal, drank a pint of whiskey, and washed it down with a bottle of ale. The door to his cell opened, and members of the Governors Rifles, a New Mexico militia, escorted Yarberry to the gallows.

Armijo marched alongside. He had been ordered to pull the lever that would send his friend, and fellow lawman, to his death, even though he had staunchly defended the condemned man throughout the trial and the entire appeals process. Even on that day, Armijo insisted that Yarberry was being unjustly hanged, the victim of local power brokers who feared that he had damaged the city's image because of his trigger-happy reputation.

In a final act of friendship, Yarberry asked that Sheriff Armijo be relieved of the unpleasant task. He requested that Sheriff Mason Bowman of Colfax County act as his replacement. Bowman refused. Count Apur, a local character, was assigned to slash the rope. Armijo asked Yarberry if he had any final words. Yarberry seized the opportunity to again proclaim his innocence, saying he was being murdered because he had killed the son of Governor Brown of Tennessee. He told the fifteen hundred spectators that he did it "in defense of my life and I was tried and acquitted but they are determined to hang Milt and they are going to do it." He used the final fifteen minutes of his life to admonish the crowd that they were going to watch an innocent man die. Then Sheriff Armijo checked his watch and gave the order to cut the rope.

Milton Yarberry was declared dead at 3:09 p.m. on February 9, 1883. The noose was still hanging around his neck when his body was placed in a simple wooden coffin and buried in the Catholic cemetery.

CHAPTER ELEVEN

José Chavez y Chavez:
The Policeman Desperado

José Chavez y Chavez led an interesting life. He escaped from a burning house with Billy the Kid. He rustled cattle. He outshot the man who killed Jesse James. He was involved in the murder of a sheriff, fought in the Lincoln County War, served as a policeman, and was accused of murdering a prisoner in his jail cell. He helped lynch a man, assisted in the murder of his employer, and was twice sentenced to death by hanging.

But he died of old age, while holding the hand of a man he had once attempted to kill.

Like many of his contemporaries, Chavez worked both sides of the law. By the time he was twenty-five, he had married, served as a constable and a justice of the peace, and helped form the Regulators, a band of deputized cowboys that played a brief, but key, role in the Lincoln County conflict.

By the time he was forty-four, he had been tried, convicted, sentenced to death, granted a new trial, sentenced to death again, spared the death penalty, and given a term of life imprisonment. But twelve years later, he was a free man.

Born in New Mexico Territory's Valencia County in 1851, Chavez migrated to Lincoln County when he was eighteen and took up residence in San Patricio, a small Hispanic village. He married Maria Lucero in January 1871; they had two daughters, Adecasio and Beatriz. He was elected precinct constable in September 1874 and was voted in as justice of the peace a year later. He was serving in both capacities when he became involved in the Lincoln County War—fought over economic control of the area— by helping found the Regulators in 1878.

The Regulators consisted of about forty men seeking vengeance for the death of John Tunstall, one of the principals in the bloody

José Chavez y Chavez had his photo taken before entering prison.
SCOTTSDALE CC SOUTHWEST STUDIES

warfare. In one of their major acts, they ambushed and killed Sheriff William Brady and his deputy on the streets of Lincoln.

The Regulators existed for only about five months, until the death of Alexander McSween, Tunstall's partner. Billy the Kid was a member but was not considered a driving force. He, Chavez, and three other Regulators were trapped in McSween's house when gunmen from the Dolan-Murphy faction set fire to it. McSween and four others died in the battle, but four of the Regulators, including Chavez and Billy, escaped out a back door. Later, Billy and Chavez were given a promise of immunity if they would agree to testify at a court of inquiry into the army's alleged lack of accountability that resulted in McSween's death. They were housed in the Lincoln County jail. During that time, a convicted murderer held in the same jail was killed, and Chavez was generally regarded as the assassin. But no charges were filed, and he and Billy were released. They both quit the Regulators within days.

Chavez then enlisted in the Lincoln County Militia, also known as the Lincoln County Mounted Rifles. Governor Lew Wallace organized the force in the hope that it might stop the widespread cattle rustling, as well as keep peace in the county. It didn't, and the group disbanded within three months. Relying on his previous experience as a lawman, Chavez ran for constable of Lincoln in 1880. He lost, primarily because of the allegations that he had killed the man in jail.

After Billy the Kid's death in July 1881, Chavez left Lincoln and wandered from place to place in New Mexico before settling in Las Vegas. Once there, his reputation with a six-gun led to his encounter with Bob Ford, who had located in the community around 1884, a couple of years after shooting Jesse James in the back.

Ford and his brother, Charley, attempted to claim the reward money offered for James's death but instead were charged with first-degree murder. They were indicted, pleaded guilty, and were sentenced to hang, but almost immediately after the sentence was pronounced, they were given a full pardon. The brothers received only a fraction of the reward money, so they were forced to eke out a meager living by reenacting the murder in a traveling road show. Bob Ford also earned extra income by posing for photographs in dime museums as the man who killed James. Neither venture was well received. When Charley Ford committed suicide in May 1884, Bob moved to Las Vegas. He and a partner opened a saloon and by 1885, he was hired as a city policeman. While serving as a lawman, according to local lore, Ford was goaded into a shooting contest with Chavez. They placed a coin on a signpost and took turns shooting at it. Ford missed by a wide margin; Chavez drew his pistol and, without aiming, hit the coin. Ford claimed the match was unfair, so Chavez challenged him to a duel with loaded guns. Rather than face a man so skilled with a six-shooter, Ford fled Las Vegas.

The incident may have been responsible for Chavez getting another job as a lawman because he was named one of three policemen in the city's Old Town soon afterward. But he couldn't shake his past life on the other side of the law. And that led him into an association with Vicente Silva.

Most residents of Las Vegas considered Silva a successful businessman, family man, and upstanding citizen. He and his wife, the former Telesfora Sandoval, arrived in Las Vegas in 1875. Before that, the couple operated a grocery store in San Pedro, a New Mexican mining town. Once established in Las Vegas, Silva opened the Imperial Saloon, which featured billiards and a dance hall, along with the usual bar. He welcomed Gabriel Sandoval, his wife's brother, into his family and gave him a job tending bar. Sandoval also acted as a part-time guardian to the abandoned child the Silvas had adopted because Telesfora was unable to have children. They named her Emma, and she was the pride of Vicente's existence.

Tall and handsome, Silva was the epitome of a good family man and business owner. He was born and raised in poverty, so wealth and prosperity brought him confidence and charisma. Therefore, he soon adapted to his new lifestyle and became one of the city's leading citizens.

But it was all a facade. Money and the good life slowly turned Silva into a vicious and hardened criminal, and his saloon soon became a front for his all-consuming greed. He surrounded himself with cruel and heartless men who went by such aliases as "the Moor," "Toothless," "the Ape," and "Pugnose." One of his more valuable employees was "the Owl," a small cross-eyed man. Because of his inconspicuous appearance, he was able to serve as Silva's spy, casually loitering around town while picking up information about possible enemies.

Silva maintained a good front. He smiled and listened to the townspeople, took part in community affairs, often donated money to charitable causes, and offered to help those who encountered problems with local government. But behind their backs he organized gangs of merciless cutthroats who waged a relentless campaign of rustling, robbery, and murder. One outfit was La Sociedad de Banditos (Society of Bandits); the other was Las Gorras Blancas (White Caps). Both were associated with El Partido del Pueblo Unido (People's Party), which served as a political front. The Bandits were a well-organized crime syndicate; the White Caps used intimidation, assault, fence cutting, and arson to drive settlers from public lands. The masked White Caps and Bandits burned crops and buildings, tore up railroad tracks, and terrorized the area. Sometimes, the gangs justified their mayhem by claiming that they were atoning for the loss of property that was supposedly taken illegally by wealthy Hispanics, who were benefiting from the breakup of communal land. Most of the time, however, it was all done to line Silva's pockets.

Considering his background, José Chavez y Chavez fit right in. He was a gunslinger, loyal to no one except those who were paying him.

And Vicente Silva was his kind of boss. Silva was cunning and ruthless, and his men followed his orders without question. So when an area rancher openly accused him of rustling horses, Silva called a clandestine meeting. He had secretly purchased a ranch in a remote and inaccessible area hidden by mining operations and used it as a storage site for rustled livestock. The rancher found it, retrieved his stolen horses, and stormed into Silva's saloon to make the accusation. Silva denied it, but the accusation shook his confidence. He figured there had to be a traitor among his collection of outlaws. During the secret meeting, held upstairs over the bar, he fingered Patricio Maes as the informer.

Maes had recently posted notice that he was leaving the People's Party to become a Republican. (The People's Party was originally formed by two Las Vegas brothers. Members rode around the territory, threatening to punish anyone they believed had illegally taken property owned by the poor peasants who farmed the land under grants given decades earlier when the territory was under Spanish control. Although they made threats and burned buildings, the group never physically attacked anyone. But when one of the founding brothers was murdered, the party fell apart due to lack of leadership. Silva had recognized it as an opportunity. He contacted the members and offered them work as rustlers, thieves, and murderers. Most of them accepted. Silva renamed them the White Caps; locals referred to them as the Forty Thieves.)

Having one of his carefully laid plans threatened by an underling, Silva considered it an affront when Maes announced his intention to leave. Silva was determined to take his revenge on the man he considered a turncoat, so the secret meeting was to serve as a mock trial. Silva appointed himself judge and named two of his men to act as attorneys, one to prosecute the alleged crime; the other to defend Maes. Although neither had any legal experience, both went about their duties with considerable enthusiasm. The discussions led to arguments, and the arguments almost produced fistfights because the accused man had friends who supported him and enemies who wanted him out of the way. And they were all Silva's men.

When the first fake trial resulted in a mixed verdict, Silva stopped the proceedings and brought in a gallon of whiskey, which was distributed among the phony jurors. The second verdict was unanimous. Maes was to be executed.

On the night of October 22, 1892, Silva ordered Chavez and his two fellow policemen, Eugenio Alarid and Julian Trujillo, to carry out the whiskey-driven decision. They threw a noose around the condemned man's neck and dragged him to an iron bridge that spanned the Gallinas River. Silva himself tied one end of the rope to a girder, and then he and a loyal follower hoisted the condemned man up and threw him over the bridge railing. Although skilled at murder, robbery, and other crimes, the gang wasn't well versed in the art of execution. As a result, the knot holding the noose to the girder was too loose; it slipped and Maes fell to the ice below.

Two of Silva's men climbed down the riverbank onto the ice and threw the loose end back to their associates, who hauled Maes back up and left him dangling in the winter chill. The next morning, residents of Las Vegas woke up to the sight of a Maes's body twisting in the wind. The *Las Vegas Optic* devoted one sentence to the murder: "Patricio Maes was taken by a mob early Saturday morning and hanged from the Gallinas River bridge at Las Vegas."

But the killing had just begun.

Although he professed his innocence, Silva was brought to trial on the rustling charge. But he provided an airtight alibi, and the charge was dropped. The incident made him extremely cautious, however, and he developed paranoia, as well as a deep mistrust for his brother-in-law, Gabriel Sandoval. Because he tended bar at the saloon, Sandoval was probably aware of Silva's misdeeds. At least, it seemed that way to Silva. So he had to be dealt with.

Also, a vigilante group, the Sociedad de Mutua Protección, or Mutual Protection Society, had started looking into Silva's activities. He didn't fear any trouble from the local police because they were all his employees, but he had no control over the vigilantes. It was time to leave town. Accompanied by several gang members, he went into seclusion, choosing a cave as his hideout. It was only twelve miles from Las Vegas, so Silva could sneak back into town at night to confer with his gangs and see the mistress he had openly kept for years.

And he could plot the removal of Gabriel Sandoval as a potential threat.

Meanwhile, a heartbroken Telesfora was forced to find work as a waitress to support herself and Emma, who was studying at Las Vegas Academy. Although abandoned by her husband, she was still madly in love with him. But she and her daughter would soon become victims of Silva's calculated plots to stay out of jail.

In a complicated maneuver that required both cunning and cruelty, Silva ordered his men to kidnap Emma. He hoped the move would scare Sandoval into silence because of his love for Telesfora, his sister, and Emma, his niece. To set the plan in motion, he ordered one of his henchmen to drive to the academy and get Emma on the pretense that he was taking her to lunch. Instead, he delivered her to Silva, who took her to Taos. Once there, he enrolled her in a local school and told her it was for her own safety. When Telesfora discovered her child was missing, she became frantic and went to the authorities. Word got back to Silva, and he became worried that she might reveal his hiding place, even though she wasn't sure where it was. In an effort to calm her, Silva sent his three policemen—Chavez, Alarid, and Trujillo—to Sandoval on the pretense that they knew where Emma was hidden and that he could help them rescue her. Sandoval told his sister what he was doing.

Sandoval accompanied the trio to an abandoned mill outside of Las Vegas, where Silva was waiting. Once there, they held his arms while Silva stabbed him to death. The policemen then carried the body back into town, stripped it, and threw it into a privy.

But the crooked cops and their leader still weren't done. Silva planned to leave for Mexico with his mistress, but he needed money. So he and his associates broke into a Las Vegas store and stole the safe. The robbery netted them only twenty-five dollars. Even worse, legitimate authorities suspected Silva and his men in the theft and put out reward notices. Now a wanted man and desperate, Silva sent a message to his wife, telling her that both her daughter and her brother were safe and that she was to pack up all her belongings and join them at his ranch. Distraught over the disappearances of her daughter and her brother, Telesfora agreed.

One of Silva's henchmen drove the frightened woman to the ranch, where Silva and three gang members waited. Instead of welcoming her with open arms, Silva roughly shoved her inside the ranch house, where he threatened her and demanded all her money. She gave him two hundred dollars; he insisted she also turn over her jewelry. When she refused, Silva stabbed her to death, dragged her body to the edge of an arroyo, and threw it down the steep embankment. He jumped on the rim of the arroyo and caused it to collapse, burying the body. Satisfied that he could now make his escape, he gave each gang member ten dollars for their troubles. It was a fatal mistake.

Shocked and angered over the murder and the measly ten-dollar payoff, Antonio José Valdez killed Silva with a single bullet to the head. The gang members threw his body next to his wife's in the arroyo, covered it with loose dirt, and rode off to split all the ill-gotten gains.

Silva's death didn't stop the White Caps, however. They continued a pattern of murder and rustling even without their leader. But the resurgence was brief. A year later, Governor William T. Thornton offered rewards and pardons to anyone who came forward with information on the disappearance of Silva, his wife, and Gabriel Sandoval or any other crimes committed during the Silva-led reign of terror. The beginning of the end came on April 10, 1894, when Manuel Gonzales y Baca, a former gang member, was arrested for his part in the lynching of Patricio Maes. He implicated Chavez, Alarid, and Trujillo in the murder of Sandoval. Alarid and Trujillo were arrested, tried, and given life sentences. Chavez fled, but after a five-hundred-dollar reward was offered, he was arrested in Socorro on May 26, 1894, while using the alias of Joe Gonzales.

A year after that, Guadalupe Caballero, the man known as "the Owl," went to authorities and revealed how Gabriel Sandoval, Telesfora Silva, and Vicente Silva had been killed. On March 17, 1895, Antonio José Valdez, the man who had fired the bullet into Vicente Silva's head, took a party led by the mayor of Las Vegas to the site.

The revelations were big news. The townspeople were relieved, and the *Las Vegas Optic* noted that "Silva was the leader of a gang of cutthroats who made so much trouble in this county two years ago. ... It is understood that Silva was murdered to obtain money supposed to be in his possession and his wife was killed to keep her from informing on the murderers."

The truth came out later, during testimony given during the trials that followed.

Chavez was accused, tried, found guilty of first-degree murder, and sentenced to death. However, before the sentence could be carried out, the territorial Supreme Court granted him a new trial. It made little difference; the outcome was the same. This time, Chavez's execution date was scheduled for October 29, 1897. But he was granted a stay of execution. Less than a month later, Governor Miguel Otero rejected the challenges and objections of the citizens of Las Vegas and commuted Chavez's death sentence to lifetime imprisonment. Otero said he felt compelled to take the unpopular action because of the publicity given the case and public pressure from outside Las Vegas to spare Chavez's life.

In early November 1897, José Chavez y Chavez became Inmate No. 1089 in the territorial penitentiary in Santa Fe, destined to spend the rest of his life behind bars. However, while serving his time, Chavez saved the life of a guard during a prison riot. The good deed did not go unnoticed. On January 11, 1909, Governor George Curry pardoned him, citing his role in quelling the prison rebellion. He returned to Las Vegas, where he worked odd jobs until his health failed. His mental health also seemed to be deserting him, because he started making some rather outrageous claims about his earlier life of crime. One claim was that he was responsible for the deaths of Colonel Albert Jennings Fountain, a prominent attorney, and his young son. Nobody believed him, and his claim was deemed highly unlikely.

José Chavez y Chavez died of natural causes in 1924, a short time before his seventy-third birthday. His wife had died years before, and his daughters allegedly lost contact with him after his criminal activities became public knowledge.

So as the old gunfighter lay on his deathbed, only Liberato Baca, a former enemy who once survived a shoot-out with the fearsome lawman/bandit, sat with him and held his hand. They had faced each other in the Lincoln County War, and Baca was considered the only man ever to square off against Chavez and live to tell about it.

CHAPTER TWELVE

The Execution of Paula Angel:
Many Men against One Woman

There was little doubt that Paula Angel was guilty. She killed her boyfriend in a fit of passion and was arrested at the scene of the crime, still holding the bloody knife used to commit the murder. When put on trial, she showed no emotion and made little attempt to defend herself against the charge. She was sentenced to death by hanging, and the execution was carried out.

But there were extenuating circumstances, coupled with miscarriages of justice, that at a later time would most certainly have spared her life, although perhaps not a lengthy prison term. She was betrayed by her lover, tormented by her jailer and prosecuted by a vengeance-minded court, denied appeals, and deprived of a legal technicality that might have saved her. Also, the local newspapers never covered her case, which meant her situation was never given the benefit of public opinion, normally a determining factor in such cases. Without that, she had no one to champion her cause.

So in her particular situation, the men in Paula Angel's life made her a victim as well as a murderer.

Her story is not as well documented as those who gained most of the notoriety in New Mexico's early history. Nobody is certain about her age, her background, or even her real name. What is certain, however, is that she was the first and only woman ever executed in New Mexico since it became a territory, then a state. And that she almost cheated death.

Historians have recorded her name as Pablita Sandoval, Paula Martin, and the generally accepted Paula Angel. She may have been as young as nineteen or as old as twenty-six when she was put to death on April 26, 1861, for a crime committed about a month earlier.

Before that, she was one of the more sought-after young women in Las Vegas. Young and beautiful, with dark flashing eyes, she came from the more upscale section of town, and men of all ages tried to become her suitors. But she refused them all until she met Juan Miguel Martin, who was married and the father of five children. He was also the son of a wealthy and well-connected Santa Fe politician. What followed was a case of history repeating itself since time immemorial: Paula fell in love and submitted to his advances.

The next part is also as old as recorded history: Martin grew tired of his conquest.

He told Paula he wanted to end the affair and go back to his family. He also began patronizing the scantily clad women who plied their trade along Sodomia, La Calle de la Amargura (the Road of Suffering and Bitterness). At the time, it was the city's bawdiest district, where ladies of the evening offered themselves in dives, saloons, cantinas, and gambling dens. When Paula learned of her boyfriend's dalliances, she begged him to meet her in front of one of the cantinas that lined the city streets.

They met and embraced. Those who saw them said it initially appeared they were trying to patch up a lovers' quarrel. But suddenly, Martin screamed in agony and fell backward. There was another scream, and he dropped to the ground. Witnesses would later testify that they saw him clutching his chest as he recoiled from the thrust of the knife Paula was holding. As he was falling, they swore in court, she stabbed him again, this time in the back.

While some bystanders rushed to the scene and grabbed Paula to stop her from another assault with the knife, others carried the wounded man into the cantina. Paula was calm, offered no resistance, and made no attempt to escape as they detained her until Sheriff Antonio Abad Herrera arrived and made the arrest. Martin died within five minutes, so Paula was immediately charged with murder.

The trial was held in San Miguel County District Court in Las Vegas, with Judge Kirby Benedict presiding. Witnesses gave damning testimony, vividly detailing how they saw Paula withdraw the knife blade from her lover's midsection, then plunge it into his back as he turned. Her lawyer defended her on the grounds that it was a crime of passion brought on by her lover's unfaithfulness. It did little good. The trial lasted less than one day. After hearing the arguments from both sides, the jurors left the room. They returned about thirty minutes later with a verdict: guilty of murder in the first degree.

Judge Benedict didn't hesitate to pass a sentence of death by hanging. He set the execution date as April 26, 1861, between the hours of 10 a.m. and 4 p.m. at a site not more than one mile from Our Lady of Sorrows of the Meadows Church. He also ordered Paula to pay all court costs. Once the sentence was delivered, Judge Benedict hustled out of town and returned to his office in Santa Fe. Although the punishment may have appeared harsh, considering the circumstances, the judge's ruling was in strict accordance with territorial law at the time. The death penalty was mandatory for all capital offenses, and first-degree murder was unequivocally a capital offense. However, many of those sentences were never carried out. Governors frequently stepped in and ordered executive clemency. They commuted death sentences to life imprisonment and, in some rare cases, the accused were actually pardoned, usually by an executive decree.

Paula Angel was granted none of these. In fact, on April 3, 1861, Governor Abraham Rencher issued the writ that ordered her death. It read, in part:

> You are ordered that on the 26th of April of 1861, you take the said Paula Angel from the jail of the County of San Miguel, in which she now finds herself incarcerated, to some appropriate place within the limits of said county, and within a distance of one mile from the seat of that county ... you then and there hang the said Paula Angel by the neck until she is dead, dead, dead, and may God have mercy on her soul.

Las Vegas was a crime-ridden town when Paula Angel was hanged there for murdering her lover.
LAS VEGAS CITIZENS COMMITTEE FOR HISTORIC PRESERVATION

She was ordered held in solitary confinement, in a small cell with only one window high above the floor. Then her torment began at the hands of Sheriff Herrera. He allowed her family only three-minute visits, and they had to converse with Paula through the small window, positioned to prevent face-to-face contact. Paula refused many of her meals and suffered daily taunts from the sheriff, who came to her cell and said, "I am going to hang you by the judge's orders until you are dead, dead, dead." Then he would remind her how many days were left until April 26.

She lost so much weight that revenge-bent law officials feared she might not live long enough to be hanged. Her attorney, Spruce Baird, filed appeals, but all were denied because the authorities were determined to see her executed and their need for revenge was stronger than his pleas for mercy. And the sheriff's taunts continued.

Another factor also worked against her. Her trial and sentence received little, if any, coverage in the frontier press. This was unusual. A woman was about to be hanged, possibly for the first time ever in the territory. It was the type of story newspapers of that era would go to battle with their competition to report, often with limited degrees of accuracy but excessive amounts of journalistic drama. Such indifference, or unawareness, undoubtedly cost Paula the powerful ally of public opinion, which might have brought pressure to bear against those involved. Pressure from an outraged public probably held more weight on such cases than it does now, because territorial authorities hated the furor and revulsion associated with the execution of a woman, guilty or not.

But the press was more concerned with the start of the Civil War and reports of huge silver strikes in Colorado, so Paula's story was completely overlooked. It wasn't fully reported until a century later, when *The New Mexican* magazine published "Bizarre Frontier Hanging Recalled," an article written by Ernie Thwaites. It detailed the circumstances surrounding the execution, as told to the reporter by a district judge who had studied the case.

But none of that mattered on April 26, 1861. Paula Angel was going to die.

A large crowd consisting of people from all over the territory gathered in Las Vegas that morning, intent upon witnessing the hanging. They watched as Sheriff Herrera loaded the frail woman into the back of a horse-drawn wagon and made her stand in the wooden coffin built to hold her body. Then they followed as he drove to a grove of cottonwood trees. He had already selected the hanging tree by throwing a noose over one limb. When the wagon and the morbid entourage following it arrived at the tree, the lawman jockeyed the wagon into place directly under the noose, and stopped the horses. He got out, climbed into the back of the vehicle, and placed the loop around Paula's neck. Then he climbed back into the driver's seat and whipped the team so it jerked away immediately, leaving the convicted woman dangling from the tree branch.

But Herrera had made two mistakes. He had forgotten how much weight Paula had lost, and he neglected to tie her hands behind her back, as was customary. So when he looked back to view his work, he saw Paula struggling to free herself. She had grabbed the rope around her neck with both hands and was trying to pull herself upward so she could slip the noose over her head. Herrera reacted instantly and raced back to the tree, grabbed Paula's waist, and tried to pull her downward so the hangman's knot could carry out its deadly assignment.

It was too much for even the most cold-hearted spectator. The crowd rushed forward, threw the sheriff to the ground, and cut the rope to release his intended victim. Herrera protested loudly that he was only trying to carry out the judge's orders; the crowd responded that, technically at least, the sentence had been carried out. Paula Angel had already been hanged.

But her fate was sealed once again, and this time the final blow was administered by an unlikely source. During the ensuing commotion, José D. Sena, a prominent Santa Fe civil servant and noted public speaker, stepped forward to address the crowd. He quoted from the death warrant and pointed out that it declared that Paula should be "hanged by the neck until dead." Therefore, he said, the bungled attempt did not comply with the strict letter of the law. His oratory quieted the crowd, and Herrera went back to work. He lifted Paula back into the bed of the wagon, tied her hands behind her back, and repeated the initial process. It worked this time, and Paula Angel earned a spot in New Mexico's history.

Later that day, Sheriff Herrera wrote his report on the back of the warrant issued by Governor Rencher. It read, *"Retornado y cumplido este mandato* (returned and completed this sentence), *hoy, Abril 26 de 1861."*

Prompted by historians' inquiries, the question of whether Paula was the first and only woman ever hanged in New Mexico arose several years later. Their research showed that two Cochiti women, Maria Joséfa and her daughter, Maria Francisca, were hanged together in 1779 for the premeditated murder of Francisca's husband. However, the area was under Spanish rule at the time, and New Mexico didn't become a territory of the United States until decades later, so the dubious honor remained with Paula.

Several other women were executed by hanging in other states, however. From the time of Paula's death until 1900, twenty-six women met their death in that fashion in the United States. Over the next thirty-seven years, another eight died on the gallows, the last in 1937 when Mississippi hanged Mary Holmes for murder. The first woman ever hanged in the country was Jane Champion, executed in New England in 1632 on an unknown charge. All told, in the United States there are 306 verified cases of women who were executed by hanging. Murder was the charge for 211 of them; 26 died after being convicted of witchcraft; one received the death sentence for adultery; and several others were hanged for bearing illegitimate children. Among the victims were Mary Latham, convicted of adultery in Massachusetts in 1643; Mary Dyer, hanged in Boston in 1660 for refusing to accept religious beliefs; Lavinia Fisher, convicted of murder in Charleston, South Carolina, whose last words were, "If you have any message for the devil, give it to me, for I am about to meet him"; and Mary Surratt, hanged by the military in Washington, D.C., on July 7, 1865, for her role in the assassination of President Abraham Lincoln.

In neighboring Arizona, the death of Eva Dugan by hanging was so gory and upsetting that the state immediately banned execution by noose. Dugan, a former cabaret entertainer in Alaska, was convicted of murdering her employer. After killing the man, she buried his body in a shallow grave, stole his car, and fled to New York. After her arrest in that state, she was extradited to Arizona where she was tried, convicted, and sentenced to death.

On February 21, 1930, she was led to the gallows. She joked with the guards but declined the opportunity to make a final statement. The trapdoor flung open, and she plunged to an instant death because her head was ripped from her body and rolled to an area where the witnesses were sitting. Within months, the state legislature enacted a law that ended legal hanging and replaced it with the gas chamber as the state's method of execution.

But back in 1861, the vengeful mind-set of the Las Vegans didn't disappear. Fifteen years after the death of Paula Angel, the citizens erected a windmill in the center of town. For a brief time, it served as a vigilante gallows where suspected criminals were sent dangling to their dooms. But a bandstand replaced that symbol of frontier justice in 1880, and the square block area was converted into a town plaza. Today, the plaza is shaded by old trees and surrounded by buildings displaying a curious mélange of architectural designs that range from Greek Revival to neoclassical.

Paula Angel's grave was located near the plaza for a while, but it vanished without a trace.

Judge Benedict, the man who ordered her death sentence, became recognized as "a man of contradictions who tried conscientiously to perform the duties entrusted to him." He earned his degree in Illinois and was a frequent companion of Abraham Lincoln when the two were starting their law careers. One newspaper report at the time praised Lincoln's cool effectiveness but noted that Benedict "was too impatient and fond of excitement to apply his energies to the acquisition of necessary legal details. ... [He] has never been a deep thinker and, in his arguments, he depends almost entirely upon the resources of a rich and powerful imagination."

He was only the fifth judge appointed to New Mexico's territorial court, where his legal opinions were generally well reasoned but sometimes tainted by the fact that he had a drinking problem. Because of that, his political enemies pressed charges against him and asked that he be removed from the bench. Their appeal went all the way to Lincoln, then the president of the United States, who reportedly reviewed the charges and said, "He may imbibe to excess, but Benedict drunk knows more law than all the others on the bench in New Mexico sober. I shall not disturb him."

Benedict eventually stopped drinking; when he died while walking the streets of Santa Fe in 1874, he was remembered as New Mexico's most colorful judge.

CHAPTER THIRTEEN
Clay Allison:
Gentleman Gunfighter

The St. James Hotel in Cimarron is a history buff's Nirvana. It's old, and it's haunted. Gunfighters squared off inside its walls, and some of their bullet holes are still visible in the tin ceiling. Famous people stayed there—people like Jesse James, Buffalo Bill Cody, Annie Oakley, Zane Grey, and Bat Masterson.

And Clay Allison once danced naked on the bar. That's worth noting because Allison wasn't known for his terpsichorean abilities. He walked with a limp, supposedly because he was born with a clubfoot or because he once shot himself in the foot. He was also one of the most feared gunslingers in New Mexico's history, according to fact, legend, and a plaque that hangs in the hotel lobby. The facts are that he was deadly with a gun. Legend says he was reckless and killed without remorse. The plaque lists the names of nineteen men, accompanied by an inscription declaring that several of them were slain by Allison.

Like many of the characters who populated the Old West during its most violent years, Allison was undoubtedly a killer, but he may not have been as cold-blooded as depicted in some historical accounts. He called himself "a shootist" and was very good at the trade. He boasted that he killed as many as fifteen men, but there's no historical proof to support the claim. There is, however, no doubt that he left several dead bodies behind as he rode the trails across Texas, New Mexico, and Colorado.

He could be brutal. One story says he decapitated a man and placed the head in front of a saloon. There also were claims that he helped lynch a man, then tied the body to his horse and dragged it through town. Most of his violent acts were blamed on an injury he suffered during his youth when a farm animal kicked him in

Clay Allison sat for a photo after shooting himself in the foot.
COURTESY OF EXPRESS ST. JAMES HOTEL, CIMARRON

the head. Later in life, a drinking problem would compound and exacerbate his belligerent attitude.

And, although he died with his boots on, his demise was the result of a farm accident, not a shoot-out.

Until he was twenty-one years old, Allison led a rather uneventful life, working on the family farm in Waynesboro, Tennessee, where he was born Robert Clay Allison in 1840, the fourth of nine children. His father, a Presbyterian minister and farmer, died five years later. When the Civil War broke out, Allison left the farm and enlisted in the Tennessee Light Artillery in October 1861. He was discharged three months later when the medical staff observed that he was "incapable of performing the duties of a soldier because of a blow received many years ago. Emotional or physical excitement produces paroxysmals of a mixed character, partly epileptic and partly maniacal."

But eight months later, he was accepted as a recruit by the Ninth Tennessee Cavalry Regiment, serving under General Nathan Bedford Forrest. Field reports said he was an intense and fearless soldier who threatened to shoot his comrades if they retreated from the advancing Union troops. The unit surrendered in May 1865, and Forrest's men were detained as prisoners of war. A short time later, the stories that would follow Allison for the rest of his life began.

In one unverified version, Allison was tried as a Confederate spy, convicted, and sentenced to be hanged. On the eve of his execution, Allison killed a guard and escaped. Other accounts merely say he was taken prisoner but remained in a Union stockade until he was released after the war ended. He returned to the farm in Tennessee, where he joined the Ku Klux Klan and nurtured a hatred for Yankees and former slaves. Unable to deal with the fact that he had fought on the losing side during the war and that those he still considered his enemies were overrunning his homeland, Allison developed a reputation as quick-tempered and trigger-happy. He was regularly involved in violent confrontations that often led to gunfire, and he never finished second. In one of his final acts before leaving Tennessee, he killed a Union solider who came to the family home and threatened to steal all their valuables. When the intruder dropped a vase given to Mrs. Allison by her departed husband, her son calmly went to a closet, removed a rifle, and shot the man. Rather than hang around to face a lot of questions, the family left the farm and headed toward Texas.

But the migration led to another example of his extreme behavior. The family and their belongings had to cross the Red River on a ferry owned by Zachary Colbert. Allison became furious over the fare and beat Colbert almost to death, leaving him unconscious on the riverbank while the Allisons ferried themselves across the water without paying. Years later, the episode would have deadly repercussions.

Clay Allison's reputation preceded him to Texas. Stories soon circulated that he had killed as many as fifteen men, and when a newspaper published an article about his involvement in the deaths, Allison wrote a letter to the editor in which he claimed, "I have at all times tried to use my influence toward protecting the property owners and substantial men of the country from thieves, outlaws, and murderers, among whom I do not care to be classed."

He also proclaimed that he never killed anyone who didn't have it coming.

But the stories continued. In one instance, after feuding with a neighbor over water rights, Allison challenged the man to a knife fight. They dug a pit in the ground, placed a blank grave marker next to the hole, and then descended into it, each armed with a large knife. According to the terms of their macabre agreement, they would fight to the death. The winner would bury the loser in the pit and have the tombstone properly engraved. There were no reports about the outcome. Obviously, however, if there ever was such a fight, Allison didn't lose.

He did refer to such a possibility several years later while talking to a group of cowboys at a roundup encampment in Texas. According to a published report, Allison declared that gunfights were not a fair way of settling arguments. "If you want to kill a man in a neat and gentlemanly way that will give both a perfectly equal show for life," the report quoted him, "let both be put in a narrow hole in the ground that they can't get out of, their left arms securely tied together, their right hands holding bowie knives, and let them cut and cut and cut until one is down. ... That's fighting dead fair."

Despite the allegations and the facts, Allison settled down in Texas and became an excellent cowboy while working on spreads in the Brazos River area. His skills were rewarded when he hooked up with two highly influential ranchers and helped move a large herd of steers into New Mexico. For his pay, he received three hundred head of cattle. He used them to start his own ranch at the confluence of the Vermejo and Canadian Rivers and became a successful cattleman. But the old habits were hard to shake. Within months of their arrival in New Mexico, Allison and his brothers, Monroe and John, made their presence known in the nearby towns of Elizabethtown and Cimarron. During their Saturday night outbursts, they'd ride into town, tour the local saloons, and then shoot out windows, lanterns, and mirrors.

Those activities were mild, however, when compared to some of the other activities credited to Clay Allison.

In the fall of 1870, while drinking in an Elizabethtown bar, Allison was confronted by a hysterical woman who claimed that her husband, Charles Kennedy, had murdered several people at their ranch. One victim, she sobbed, was their own daughter. Enraged, Allison recruited several cowboys, and they rode to the Kennedy ranch and apprehended the alleged killer. They hog-tied the man and brought him back to town, where he was jailed. But later, when the makeshift posse found some bones buried on the ranch, they stormed back into town, dragged the man from his cell, and took him to a local slaughterhouse, where they lynched him. In a drunken rage, Allison used an ax to decapitate the corpse, threw the head into a sack, and rode twenty-six miles to Cimarron, where he impaled the head on a steel rod and placed it in front of a saloon as a warning to other would-be criminals.

Like many of the other violent acts attributed to Allison, there are inconsistencies in the story. Although Kennedy was charged with murder, a jury failed to find him guilty and another trial was ordered. But before it could be held, vigilantes broke into his makeshift jail and took him to the slaughterhouse, where he was hanged before authorities could determine whether the bones they found were human. There was never any proof that Allison was a member of the vigilantes, and the saloon where he allegedly placed the gruesome trophy wasn't built until two years after the lynching occurred.

The stories persisted, however, and later incidents would lend credibility to the theories that he was fast on the draw and quick on the trigger.

In April 1871, he and two friends were accused of stealing twelve mules owned by the US Army and selling them to area ranchers. When the trio tried it again later that year, they were spotted by soldiers, and, while scrambling to get away, Allison shot himself in the foot. He escaped but was left with a permanent limp in his injured foot that was even worse than that caused by his unscathed clubfoot. No charges were ever filed, but his reputation continued to grow.

Less than three years later, he shot and killed Chunk Colbert, a gunman who bragged he had already slain at least seven men and openly swore that Allison would be his next victim. Colbert claimed the shooting would be a matter of vengeance because he was the nephew of Zachary Colbert, the ferryman Allison had nearly beaten to death years earlier. Despite the animosity, the two met at a track in Red River and raced their horses against each other in a grudge match. When the race ended in a draw, they started drinking and agreed to have dinner together. Colbert made his move during the meal, but as he drew his gun, it hit the table-top and the shot went astray. Allison responded immediately. He fired once. The bullet hit Colbert in the head. A quickly assembled coroner's jury declared it a matter of self-defense. When a local authority asked why Allison had accepted a dinner invitation from someone who was planning to kill him, he responded, "Because I didn't want to send a man to hell on an empty stomach."

Two weeks later, Colbert's friend Charles Cooper disappeared. He had witnessed the shooting and was last seen riding out of town with Allison. Some thought Allison killed him; others speculated that he had only threatened him so Cooper fled. No body was ever found, but the case would reemerge years later.

By 1875, Allison was involved in the Colfax County War, a bloody conflict over land rights that claimed an estimated two hundred lives. The dispute pitted the powerful Santa Fe Ring, composed of wealthy landowners and corrupt public officials, against settlers, miners, and ranchers who formed a loosely knit organization known as the Colfax County Ring. The conflict erupted after the fabulously wealthy Lucien Maxwell sold his vast acreage. Maxwell had, through marriage and questionable business activities, acquired almost two million acres, which made him the largest landowner in the United States. His spread stretched from just below Cimarron north to the Colorado border. But when old age slowed him down, Maxwell sold out to a British land corporation. That group in turn sold to a Dutch conglomerate, and the new owners began forcibly removing squatters from lands they had farmed and ranched for generations.

The Santa Fe Ring supported the owners, and its self-appointed court system readily upheld their claims. Allison and the Colfax County Ring objected, and their objections led to violence. One opposition leader was the Reverend Franklin J. Tolby, a Methodist circuit rider who was an outspoken critic of the Santa Fe Ring and one of Allison's close friends. When Tolby was ambushed and killed by a suspected Santa Fe Ring assassin, Allison helped organize the posse that arrested Cruz Vega, the newly appointed Cimarron constable, and charged him with Tolby's murder. Vega avowed his innocence; nobody was listening. A mob broke into the jail, hauled the man to a nearby telegraph pole, and hanged him. In a rare act of kindness, Allison shot the victim in the back to end his suffering. But then he cut the body down, tied it to his horse, and dragged it through the streets of Cimarron and out into the desert, where he left it.

Francisco Griego, the victim's uncle, found the body the next morning and, with the help of friends and relatives, began funeral preparations. Allison followed them. He told the mourners that Vega could not be buried in the local cemetery alongside "decent folks." They tried to dig a grave outside the cemetery, but Allison again confronted them and said they couldn't hold the burial within the city limits. Finally, the group buried Vega about a half mile out of town. Soon afterward, Griego began making threats.

Accompanied by his partner, Florencio Donahue, and Vega's son, Griego found Allison drinking in the St. James Hotel. Griego made accusations; Allison kept drinking. Griego removed his hat and began fanning himself; it was meant to be a distraction while he drew his gun. Allison wasn't fooled. He shot his accuser twice. Griego died instantly. The saloon closed until an inquest could be held. Shutting off their liquor supply upset the locals more than the two deaths. Allison went on a rampage, roaming the streets and shooting out windows. Then, after returning to the saloon where he had killed Griego, he stripped naked and performed a war dance. Ten days later, he was formally charged with Griego's death, but the court ruled it was justifiable homicide and the charges were dropped.

One of his next acts was a complete reversal of form, as Allison sprang to the defense of Ada Morley, the wife of newspaper publisher William Morley. She was accused of robbing the mails and ordered to stand trial in Santa Fe. As a favor, she had intercepted a letter that might have caused trouble for a friend had it been delivered. After Allison warned that "not a man will come out of the courthouse alive" if the trial was held, the charge was dropped.

But a short time later, Morley's newspaper, the *Cimarron News and Press,* printed a scathing editorial accusing Allison of a variety of misdeeds. In retaliation, Allison and two cronies broke into the office, set off an explosion, and threw the printing press into the Cimarron River. The next day, after Ada Morley publicly reprimanded Allison for his part in the incident, he apologized and handed her two hundred dollars to pay for the damages.

By early 1876, Governor Samuel Beach Axtell, a member of the Santa Fe Ring, vowed to have Allison either indicted for murder or forced out of the county. He approved a five-hundred-dollar reward for Allison on a charge of murdering Charles Cooper, Chunk Colbert's friend who had disappeared in 1874. After riding with the governor in a stagecoach from Cimarron to Trinidad, Colorado, Allison said he would surrender if Axtell would promise him a fair trial. They reached an agreement. Allison turned himself in and went to trial in Taos. His defense was that no body had ever been found.

He was acquitted and left Colfax County, but not else much changed.

In December 1876, Allison and his brother John took to drinking in Las Animas, Colorado, and caused a ruckus in a saloon when they ordered the patrons to do the "gunshot dance," a common form of horseplay in which the dancers are forced to hop around to the accompaniment of bullets aimed at their feet. Someone called the law; Deputy Sheriff Charles Faber came to the saloon and asked the brothers to put down their firearms. When they refused, Faber left, deputized two local men, and returned, armed with a shotgun. As they came through the door, someone yelled a warning and John Allison drew his gun. Faber fired once; the blast hit John Allison in the chest. Clay Allison shot four times; all four shots hit Faber. One was fatal. Faber's shotgun discharged as he fell, and John Allison was hit again, this time in the leg. Clay chased the two deputies out of the saloon and then called for a doctor. Next, he dragged the lawman's body to his brother's side and said, "Look here, John! This is the son-of-a-bitch that shot you! Everything's going to be all right. You'll be well soon!"

Both brothers were arrested and charged with manslaughter. The charge against John was dismissed for lack of evidence. In Clay's case, a grand jury returned a verdict of not guilty on grounds of self-defense. John Allison eventually recovered.

In 1877, Allison was arrested as an accessory in the murder of three black soldiers in Cimarron. Lack of evidence caused the case to be dismissed. He moved to Kansas and became a cattle broker while furthering his temperamental reputation. While in Dodge City, he had a brush with Wyatt Earp.

According to a story related years later by Chalk Beeson, a Dodge City businessman who was there at the time, the gunslinger/cattleman arrived in Dodge looking for trouble. He confronted Earp and his deputies over what he considered mistreatment of his ranch hands. Earp claimed they were "untamed cowboys," but Allison said they were just impetuous young men having a good time.

The cowboys, led by Allison, hit almost every saloon in Dodge, and as their whiskey-fueled anger increased, so did their unwillingness to adhere to the local laws. The more they drank, the more windows they shot out. By early afternoon, the streets were filled with shooting and shouting cowboys, and the prospects for a major gunfight grew proportionately. Faced with the possibility of a confrontation with two dozen liquored-up cowpokes, Earp and his deputy began to assemble a posse and prepare for the inevitable shoot-out. But cooler heads prevailed when Beeson and Dick McNulty, another business owner, intervened and persuaded Allison and his crew to give up their guns and disperse.

According to Beeson's version, Earp and the other lawmen never showed up. Beeson said that made it look as though Allison's reputation superseded Earp's bravery. The *Dodge City Globe* tactfully observed that "it is said the officers failed to appear. These occurrences are the subjects of much comment on the conduct of the officers."

The Allison brothers, Clay and John, returned to Texas, where they married the McCullough sisters. Clay and his wife, Dora, had a daughter, which settled him down somewhat, but not completely. Once he rode nude through the streets of Mobeetie, Texas, shouting that drinks in the local saloon were on him. When a lawman tried to intervene, Allison forced him into the saloon and made him drink whiskey until he was unable to stand.

While on a cattle drive in Cheyenne, Wyoming, Allison developed a toothache. He went to a local dentist who, unfortunately for him, worked on the wrong tooth. Allison stormed out of the office and found another dentist who repaired the damage. He returned to the offending dentist, threw him into a chair, and used a pair of forceps to extract one of his teeth. He was working on a second one when the man's screams alerted neighbors, who pulled his attacker away.

From 1880 to 1883, the Allison brothers ranched together in Wheeler County, Texas; Clay Allison sold out and bought another spread near the Pecos River crossing on the Texas–New Mexico line.

All the notoriety, deserved or otherwise, came to an abrupt end on July 3, 1887. Allison had driven a buckboard into Pecos, Texas, to buy supplies for his ranch. On the way home, one of the grain sacks became dislodged, and as Allison tried to stop it from falling, he lost his balance and fell under the wagon. The wheels crushed his neck, and he died on the spot.

The *Las Vegas Optic*'s story about his death read:

> *Clay Allison, a brave, true-hearted and oft-times danger-ously reckless man, when in cups, has at last died with his boots on, but not by the pistol route. He fell from his wagon in Texas some days ago, the wheel of the same running over his neck and breaking it. The team jogged on into the distance and left him lying there, dead and alone in the prairie.*

He was buried in the Pecos cemetery. Hundreds attended his funeral, either out of curiosity, friendship, or relief. His second daughter was born seven months later. A special ceremony was held in August 1975 when his remains were reinterred in Pecos Park near the Pecos Museum. Two gravestones mark the site. One says, ROBERT CLAY ALLISON. GENTLEMAN GUNFIGHTER. 1840–1887. The other bears the inscription: HE NEVER KILLED A MAN THAT DID NOT NEED KILLING.

CHAPTER FOURTEEN
Massai:
A Legend Shrouded in Mystery

In the 1954 movie *Apache,* actor Burt Lancaster portrays Massai, an Apache warrior. In this big-screen version of his life, the US Army relentlessly pursues Massai because he refuses to surrender his freedom and be forcibly relocated to a reservation. But he manages to elude the troops until near the end of the production. At that point, according to the movie, he has settled down with his wife, started a family, and become a farmer. All ends happily when the army realizes that he is no longer a threat and marches away, leaving the hero with his kin and corn crop.

Typical of filmed biographies, *Apache* got some of the names right but most of the facts wrong. The portrayal is historically sketchy, at best, and the ending is complete fiction.

The original screenplay, based on Paul Wellman's novel *Bronco Apache,* called for the army to kill Massai. But Lancaster and United Artists didn't like the downbeat final scene so they rewrote it and shot another ending. Robert Aldrich, the director, fought against the change but lost that battle to Lancaster and studio executives. Aldrich stayed on as director because, as he recalled later, "once Burt had changed his mind, it made little difference if I refused to direct the other ending because the next day they would have gotten someone who would."

Such was life in the reel world.

In real life, there was an Apache warrior named Massai. He did become a renegade, fleeing from the federal government that ordered him to confinement on a Florida reservation. And the army did spend a lot of time chasing him.

But they never caught him.

And, although others would claim that they either apprehended him or killed him, Massai's eventual fate remains one of those tantalizing mysteries that will probably never be solved to the complete satisfaction of those who study such things.

There are those who claim that his life ended in New Mexico during a shoot-out with a band of cowboys. There are others who say he died of tuberculosis. And some adhere to the story that he escaped into Mexico and lived with a group of rebels. Long after his death, his daughter related her version; it was disputed by historians. So, outside of the fact that he never actually became a farmer, nobody knows for sure how his story ended.

Massai, born in southern New Mexico Territory sometime between 1847 and 1860, was also known as Massa, Massi, Masai, Wasse, or Ma-si. He was a member of the Mimbres band of Chiricahua Apache and remained near his birthplace until 1877, when he and his people were forcibly removed from their homeland and placed on the San Carlos Reservation near Globe in the Arizona Territory. Although there under protest, he married, had children, and served in an Apache police and scout troop commanded by a white US Army officer.

Five years after the relocation, his unit was sent to New Mexico on a brief assignment and then ordered back to San Carlos. During the train ride back, Massai learned that his wife and children had been taken captive by Juh, a Chiricahua leader. Juh, who fled from federal authorities rather than submit to reservation life, had led a raid from his stronghold in Mexico and swept into San Carlos, abducting several Mimbres, including Massai's family, to serve in his army.

Near panic, Massai jumped from the train and walked to Mexico. He eventually caught up with Juh and his captives and was reunited with his wife and children. He stayed with the renegades for a while, then stole a horse, left the captors, and headed north. Jason Betzinez, a member of Juh's band, encountered Massai during his brief stay in Mexico. When his recollections were published in 1959 in a book entitled *I Fought with Geronimo*, Betzinez said Massai was "one of those restive individuals who could not stay long in one place [and] he seemed to have a distaste for the rest of us, possibly because we were outlaws."

Burt Lancaster portrayed Massai in the 1956 movie Apache.

Although he abhorred reservation life, Massai went back to San Carlos and was readmitted to his unit, where he served alongside Haskay-Bay-Nay-Ntayl, better known as the Apache Kid. He was still a scout with the army in 1886, when Geronimo and his band made their final surrender to General Nelson Miles. Geronimo and those who rode and fought with him were unceremoniously loaded into railroad boxcars and shipped to a Florida reservation. A short time later, a new order declared that Massai and all the other Indian scouts, along with their families, were also to be incarcerated, even though they had served the army faithfully. The Apache Kid wasn't among them; he had been convicted of attempted murder and was sentenced to a term in Yuma Territorial Prison, but he escaped while being transferred there from the jail in Globe. Massai and the Kid would later become inextricably linked through accusations and deeds.

During the time Massai and the Apache Kid worked for the military, Al Sieber was the US Army's chief of scouts, a position he held because he knew the ways of the Apache. He was wounded while serving with the First Minnesota Volunteer Infantry during the Civil War and took another bullet in 1875, during a battle against the Apaches in Arizona. More than a decade later, he suffered another wound during a fracas at San Carlos, and that injury spelled doom for the Apache Kid.

The Apache Kid was born along the Gila River in Arizona Territory around 1859. His family was part of a peaceful band led by Capitan Chiquito, living in the serenity of Aravaipa Canyon. But the area lost its innocence in 1872, when President Ulysses S. Grant ordered the establishment of the San Carlos Reservation and ordered all Apaches, regardless of tribal affiliation, to move there. A year later, silver was discovered in the area and the lives of the Apaches were forever changed, as the usual assortment of miners, saloon keepers, prostitutes, and criminals arrived to make their fortunes, one way or another.

The boy who would become the Apache Kid adjusted to the changes caused by the influx of strangers and eventually met

Sieber, who determined that the youngster had leadership qualities and signed him up for his scout corps. By this time, he was known simply as "the Apache Kid," rather than his given name. Sieber trusted him, and the trust was well rewarded. The Apache Kid performed well on several excursions with the army and was elevated in rank. However, one night in May 1887, Sieber left him in charge of the reservation guardhouse while he and another military official left the reservation to attend to military business. It was a mistake. The Apache Kid had an old score to settle with a brother of the man who had killed his father. Although the killer was caught and executed by the tribe, the Apache Kid believed the brother had also been involved. It was a matter of tribal "eye for an eye" justice, and he believed it was his duty to carry it out. So he left the reservation and took care of the matter with a single shot.

Sieber was furious and had the Apache Kid arrested, along with five other scouts. However, a riot broke out among other Apaches who thought the arrests were unjust because, they believed, tribal law superseded the white man's rules, so the death was justifiable. During the uprising, Sieber was shot in the leg. The wound left him with a permanent limp. The Apache Kid and the five others fled but surrendered a few weeks later. Sieber was among their accusers at the trial. All six were found guilty of mutiny and desertion and sentenced to death. After intervention by General Nelson Miles, who claimed the court didn't understand tribal laws, the sentences were reduced to prison time. The Apache Kid got ten years in federal prison and was sent to Alcatraz. After serving less than a year, however, his case was examined by a review board, which concluded that the jurors were prejudiced against Apaches, so the sentence was thrown out.

But the reversal did not lead to a happy ending.

The Apache Kid returned to San Carlos, where he faced more court decisions. Eventually, he was charged with federal crimes, among them "attempting to kill Al Sieber." A new jury heard Sieber testify that, although he knew the Apache Kid was not the one who shot him, he held him responsible for the wound that left him disabled. The jurors agreed, found the Apache Kid guilty, and sentenced him to seven years in the territorial prison in Yuma.

He never got there.

On November 2, 1889, the Apache Kid and eight other prisoners were loaded onto a stagecoach in Globe to begin the journey to Yuma. Sheriff Glenn Reynolds led the entourage. He knew the road well, so he was aware that the stage probably couldn't navigate a steep incline known as the Kelvin Grade with a full load of passengers. He also feared that a snowstorm was forming, which would further complicate the treacherous climb. So he ordered seven of his prisoners to get out and walk behind while he and his deputy, William "Hunkydory" Holmes, brought up the rear with their guns primed for firing should there be trouble. The Apache Kid and another prisoner stayed in the coach while driver Eugene Middleton maneuvered it up the slope.

Because they were armed, Reynolds and his deputy felt safe. But as soon as the stagecoach disappeared over the hill, six of the convicts walking behind encircled and overpowered the two lawmen. Some of them beat Holmes to death with rocks, then grabbed his rifle and shot him in the head. Outnumbered and trapped, Reynolds was unable to get even one shot off before the prisoners wrestled his rifle away and turned it on him, killing him with three bullets to the chest. Middleton, the driver, heard the shots and knew there was trouble. But the others were all hidden from his view so he had no idea what was happening. Then one of the prisoners, horse thief Jesus Avott, came running up the hill and shouted a warning. But Avott didn't speak English so Middleton didn't understand what he was yelling about. Seconds later, a bullet tore through the driver's cheek while Avott fled into the brush. After the shooting was over, he took one of the stagecoach's horses and rode into Florence to sound the alarm. Middleton, realizing that he had only one chance for survival, fell to the ground and played dead. The escapees had already taken the keys from the bodies of the dead lawmen and removed their shackles; when they reached the stage, they freed the two men inside.

Two of the killers approached Middleton as he lay on the ground. One was carrying a large rock; the other had the sheriff's rifle. He aimed it at the man's head and was about to shoot when the Apache Kid ordered him to stop, saying the man was already dead so there was no reason to waste a bullet. Then they fled.

The men earlier involved with the Apache Kid, and those who escaped with him, moved on toward their fates. All those who were with the Apache Kid on the stagecoach were recaptured within ten months. Some were killed by Indian scouts; some committed suicide while in captivity. Al Sieber served as a scout on the San Carlos Reservation for more than thirty years but left after a disagreement with the military. In 1904, Sieber was employed as a foreman working on the Apache Trail, a twisting, turning, forty-mile roadway built through Arizona's Superstition Mountains to haul supplies from Phoenix to the construction site of the Roosevelt Dam. Sieber and his crew were working on a section of the road near Tonto Creek when a rock fell, crushing his legs. Although he had survived three gunshot wounds, Sieber's luck ran out this time. He died about an hour later. A monument was erected to his memory at the scene of the accident.

Avott, the convict who tried to warn Middleton about the death of the lawmen, was given a pardon for bringing news of the escape to the attention of authorities. Middleton, despite his near-fatal injury, lived for another forty years. After his death in 1929, he was buried next to the graves of Sheriff Reynolds and Deputy Holmes in Globe.

Meanwhile, the legend of the Apache Kid developed and grew. He became a veritable nightmare for those living in the central Arizona and New Mexico Territories. Apache Kid sightings became common across borders and down into Mexico. Almost every murder committed anywhere in that vast area was attributed to him, justifiably or not. Reports of his death were equally widespread, but another massacre or kidnapping usually occurred a short time later to belie the claims. He was, according to those who lived there at the time, everywhere—a ghostlike figure who moved through the deserts and mountains with little or no interference.

Meanwhile, in the near-pandemonium that followed the Apache Kid's brazen escape, the Anglo residents in the area got more bad news: Massai was also running loose.

There was a growing fear that he would team up with the Apache Kid to create havoc among the white settlers.

Like the Apache Kid, Massai escaped from custody and eluded his captors from that day forward. Although he also was well guarded, Massai never arrived in Florida. There are two versions of how he fled those who detained him.

According to one account, Massai began planning his getaway as soon as the train taking him to Florida pulled out of Fort Bowie Station in southeastern Arizona Territory. One of the other prisoners was a young woman about to give birth, and he would use that in his race to freedom. Massai reasoned that, if the baby was born during the journey to Florida, his escape wouldn't be noticed because the head tally would remain the same. Although the guards took a head count every few hours, conditions in the boxcars were so deplorable that the watchmen weren't very thorough.

Fortunately for Massai, the train was slow and frequently pulled into sidings to let other trains pass. After several hours spent waiting on the sidings, the guards relaxed their watch. So when the baby was born, the mother was able to hide it and the guards didn't notice anything unusual. Somewhere near Springfield, Missouri, the train pulled into another siding, allowing a circus train to pass. While the guards and prisoners crammed themselves to one side of the boxcar to see the circus animals, Massai slipped out the other side, hid in the weeds along the tracks, and waited there until the train pulled out. The guards didn't notice because the young mother then revealed her infant, which resulted in the head count remaining the same. Nobody realized that Massai was gone until the train reached Florida, where the head count matched but the number of warriors was one short.

In the other version of the story, Massai and Gray Lizard, a close friend, were in the same boxcar with Massai's wife and his children. She urged them to escape, and after four days, they were able to pry some boards loose and get away. After making their way back to New Mexico, they parted company, never to see each other again.

Regardless of which account is more factual, one thing was certain: Massai was loose.

So was the Apache Kid.

And now there was a growing dread that the two would team up against the settlers who occupied their homelands. Whether they did or not remains uncertain. But the possibility was so obvious that every crime perpetrated against the whites during that period was blamed on one or both of them. They were familiar with the territory, so they knew where to find hiding places and watering holes. This gave them a significant advantage over their pursuers. And the longer they stayed free, the more their feats, true or not, elevated them to legendary status.

In actuality, the two probably did cross paths but never became associates of any kind. After his escape, and guided by instinct and his will to survive, Massai traveled more than fifteen hundred miles back to his native land, somewhere west of the Mescalero Apache country in New Mexico. Although he was allowed to live with the Mescaleros, he preferred to be alone because he trusted no one, particularly white men and those Indians who accepted reservation life without complaint. His dislike for white men, fueled by the attempt to relocate him to Florida, grew into abject hatred, and he began raiding their property regularly and with a vengeance. He eluded all attempts at capture, moving only at night and hunting with a bow and arrow to avoid detection. Famed western artist Frederic Remington referred to his ghost-like elusiveness in an article he wrote for *Harper's New Monthly Magazine* in 1898. He quoted an old Apache scout, who told him: "Massai's trail was so crooked, I had to study nights to keep it arranged in my head. He didn't leave much more trail than a buzzard, anyhow, and it took years to unravel it."

His wife and children were among those shipped to Florida, and there was little hope that he would ever see them again. Eventually, the loneliness became more than even he could bear. He

The Apache Kid and Massai (pictured here) created a reign of terror together.
SAM LOWE COLLECTION

stole into San Carlos and kidnapped a young woman after killing her mother. A detachment of troops set out after them, but he used stealth, cunning, and mountain trails to avoid them. When he grew tired of the girl, he released her and she returned home. According to the old Apache scout who had confided in Remington, the girl feared her captor and justifiably so. He had threatened to kill her several times but relented and sent her back to her family. The scout told Remington that Massai later returned to San Carlos and took another girl but killed her when he was surrounded by Apache scouts and members of her tribe who tried to rescue her. He escaped, and his legend grew.

Massai confined his activities to areas near the Arizona–New Mexico border, but he would cross into Mexico whenever the troops got too close. He allegedly killed without remorse, took whatever supplies he needed from his victims, and then rode back into the mountains. After months of life as a hermit, he stole a Mescalero girl named Zanagoliche and took her to a village in New Mexico. They were married in an Apache ceremony that was not opposed by tribal members because of the assumption that Massai would never see his original family again. According to the combination of fact and legend, they had as many as six children together while being steadily pursued by the army, bounty hunters, and sheriffs' posses.

A prospector was killed near Mogollon in New Mexico, and raids continued in the same area through 1905. All were attributed to Massai. In September 1906, fed up with the increasing violence, a New Mexico posse rode into the hills, determined to end Massai's depredations. They ambushed two Indians in San Juan Canyon. One was killed, but the other escaped, leaving a trail of blood. Later that day, an Apache woman staggered into a line rider's shack, hungry and exhausted. He gave her food and alerted authorities, but she was gone when the posse arrived. They found evidence that she had hidden children nearby, but there was no sign of any of them. Days later, the woman was spotted trying to obtain food from a garbage can behind a hotel in San Marcial. Officials notified the army, and she was captured. She said she was the wife of Massai.

She told authorities that white men had killed her husband at the head of San Juan Canyon in the San Mateo Mountains and then chased her for days before she and her children got away. She was placed under guard but escaped and returned to the Mescalero Reservation, where she told the same story to the Indian agent stationed there.

But the saga wasn't over.

A story that circulated around the same time claimed that Zanagoliche retracted her initial claims and told authorities that she was actually the Apache Kid's wife and that he was the man shot dead by the posse. Apparently, it was only another piece of fiction circulated by hearsay and an unrestrained press.

However, after the death of the Indian killed by the New Mexican posse, the raids that had been going on for seventeen years suddenly stopped. This gave credibility to the Indian woman's claim that she was Massai's widow. More than fifty years later, even more proof emerged when Alberta Begay told her story to Ruidoso historian Eve Ball. Alberta Begay appeared to have good credentials because, she said, she was the daughter of Massai and Zanagoliche.

In her version, the family fled their mountain hideout because Massai had killed a man and they feared they would be captured. He told his wife and children that if anything happened to him, they should return to the Mescalero Reservation. The following morning, as he and his son Albert were checking their horses, shots rang out. The son followed his father's orders and ran. Massai fell dead. Albert raced back to the family with the news, but Zanagoliche refused to leave until she was certain her husband had been killed. When it was safe, they returned and found the remains of a campfire. When she sifted through the ashes, Zanagoliche found bones and a belt buckle, which she said belonged to Massai. They dug a shallow grave, buried the remains, and then made their way to San Marcial.

Ball's article was published in the July/August edition of *True West* in 1959. In gratitude, Alberta Begay presented the author with the belt buckle.

There were probably an equal number of versions about the death of the Apache Kid. Ed "Wallapai" Clark, an Arizona rancher, claimed that he killed the Apache Kid on his ranch in eastern Arizona. Another report claimed that a posse led by Charles Anderson shot and killed him near Kingston, a mining camp in New Mexico. Mickey Free, an army scout, once produced a piece of decomposed skin as proof that the Apache Kid was dead because the skin bore a faint mark similar to those that had been tattooed on the foreheads of all San Carlos men after they were forced onto the reservation. Another Arizona rancher, John Slaughter, maintained that he killed the Apache Kid in Mexico's Sierra Madres but didn't mention it until years later because he had crossed the Mexican border and didn't want to get into legal trouble. Still others claimed that the Apache Kid lived out his life in peace with a tribe of Apaches in Mexico.

The only certainty among all of these cases is that nobody knows the truth.

The movie version of Massai's life opened in Chicago's Roosevelt Theater, preceded by a parade that featured covered wagons and buckboards, Indians in full regalia, cowboys, and tribal ceremonies. After its nationwide release, the reviews ranged from lukewarm to unenthusiastic. The *Los Angeles Times* called it "a fine, fine picture." The *New York Times* reviewer called it a "resounding clinker." And the *Hollywood Reporter* critic commented that "somewhere during the proceedings, Mr. Lancaster says, 'The corn is talking,' and I'm afraid that about summarizes the literary aspects of the film."

CHAPTER FIFTEEN
The Ketchum Brothers:
Murderers and Train Robbers

Long before 8:00 a.m. on April 6, 1901, a crowd had gathered outside the jail in Clayton, New Mexico Territory. A historic event was about to take place, and nobody wanted to miss the excitement surrounding the final hours of Tom Ketchum, the one-armed man they called "Black Jack." This would be his last day on Earth.

For years, the mere mention of a train robbery anywhere in Texas, Arizona, and New Mexico was usually accompanied by a reference to the Ketchum brothers, Tom and Sam, and their band of outlaws. They were such skilled practitioners of the act that they looted almost at will for nearly a decade. They bragged that it was easier than tending cattle herds, it required very little hard work, and it provided them with a comfortable living.

But now their luck had run out. Sam Ketchum was already dead; Tom was ascending the steps to the gallows.

Although a man was about to die, it was not a very solemn occasion. In fact, the mood was almost festive. The saloons were open, and the bartenders were busy dispensing their frothy brews to quench the thirst of those who had come to see the first execution in the county. And, almost as a bonus, the victim was going to be Black Jack Ketchum, the man who had terrorized the area for nearly ten years. Business was also brisk on the streets of Clayton. Stores were offering souvenirs for sale; lawmen were selling tickets to those who wanted to witness the hanging close up; other vendors were peddling sticks with a doll-like representation of Black Jack hanging from them.

The crowd was orderly but anxious. The execution had been delayed several times, and Ketchum had spent twenty-one months in prison while going through the legal proceedings. After all his

Tom "Black Jack" Ketchum met a sudden death in Clayton.
HERZSTEIN MEMORIAL MUSEUM, CLAYTON, NM

appeals had been heard and denied, the original schedule called for the hanging to be carried out later in the year. Then authorities heard rumors that the Ketchum Gang was planning an attempt to free their remaining leader, so the date was moved up. Today would be the day.

Not at the designated hour, however.

Since this was the first time anyone had been scheduled to hang in Clayton, or anywhere else in Union County, local law officials were uncertain about how to do it in the accepted manner. They held discussions about both the length and the sturdiness of the rope. They weren't sure how to construct a gallows. And there were still questions about whether robbing trains was a capital offense. The territorial legislature had only recently passed the law calling for the death penalty for such crimes, and the charge against Ketchum was "felonious assault upon a railway train."

Holding up a train was a primary source of outlaw revenue at the time because it was profitable and relatively uncomplicated. And the Ketchum Gang had it down to a science. Once they selected a target, the robbers waited in ambush at a spot where the train either stopped to take on water and fuel or slowed to traverse a steep grade. Then they scrambled aboard the engine with six-guns drawn and ordered the engineer and conductor to uncouple the locomotive and express car. When those two units were safely away from the rest of the train, they blew the safe open, made off with the contents, and lived the good life until their funds ran out.

Then they did it all over again, using the same technique.

But the Ketchums didn't limit their criminal activities to robbing trains. They committed murders, held up post offices, robbed general stores and saloons, and even became involved in a murder-for-hire scheme. Their gang included other thieves, murderers, and robbers, and they terrorized the southwestern territories for more than nine years. But in the end, it led most of them to premature deaths.

Today, April 6, 1901, it would be Tom Ketchum's turn.

Earlier in the day, Ketchum boasted to his cellmates that "I'll be in hell before you start breakfast, boys." After eating his final meal, he asked the musicians who had gathered as part of the festivities to play his favorite songs, "Just as the Sun Went Down" and "Amelia Waltzes." Then, less than six months shy of his thirty-eighth birthday, he was escorted to the gallows, each step taking him closer to his last breath.

Each step taking him closer to a fate that Sam Ketchum, his older brother, had already suffered.

Sam and Tom were the sixth and seventh children born into a ranching family living near San Angelo, Texas, in the mid-1800s. Tom was eight years younger than Sam and twelve years younger than Green Berry Ketchum, the oldest brother. When their parents died, Green became the head of the family. Times were tough so the boys had to find work on neighboring cattle ranches. Sam got married, but his wife ran off with another man, taking their two children with them.

Tom also fell in love, but his intended dumped him while he was away earning enough money to buy an engagement ring. The couple held a tearful farewell before he rode off to help drive a herd of cattle to market. But at one cattle stop along the way, he received a note from his intended. In it, she wrote that the passionate good-bye was all meant to deceive him into believing that she could never love anyone but him. But, she added, as soon as Tom left town, she married another man. She signed the note with her married name.

Shortly after that, Green Ketchum started a horse ranch in Knickerbocker, Texas, and hired his brothers to help run the spread. The arrangement didn't work out. Angered by their refusal to work as hard as he wanted, Green ordered the two off his property. Now unemployed, Sam and Tom drifted across Texas, New Mexico, and Colorado, working as ranch hands and drovers.

Their first foray into crime happened in 1892, when they hooked up with a band of outlaws to hold up an Atchison, Topeka and Santa Fe train carrying a large payroll to Deming, New Mexico. They got away with about twenty thousand dollars. A conductor on the train slipped away during the robbery and alerted authorities, but by the time the posse arrived, the robbers and their loot were long gone. Nobody was arrested; none of the money was recovered.

Three years later, Tom and several associates murdered John Powers, a Texas rancher. Although he later admitted his part in the shooting, Tom said he'd been paid to do it by the rancher's wife because she was having an affair with the ranch foreman and her husband's death would simplify the situation. Tom was charged but never arrested because he and Sam had fled back to New Mexico.

Two significant events followed.

First, Tom Ketchum became "Black Jack" Ketchum. Second, the brothers organized the Black Jack Ketchum Gang.

The story of the name change has two versions, both centered on facial hair. One says the change occurred when someone told Tom that, because of his mustache, he resembled General John "Black Jack" Pershing, the US Army leader who would later pursue Pancho Villa into Mexico after he and his small army attacked Columbus, New Mexico. Although Pershing was stationed at Fort Bayard, New Mexico, for a time during the Ketchum gang's reign of terror, he himself didn't acquire the nickname until he was appointed to the West Point tactical staff as an instructor in 1897.

The other, and probably more accurate, account says it happened after Will "Black Jack" Christian, another outlaw working the same area, was killed by a posse near Clifton, Arizona Territory. A telegram sent to New Mexico authorities said that "Black Jack killed by our posse yesterday" and a second wire identified the dead man as Tom Ketchum. Since there was also a marked resemblance between the two, primarily due to their mustaches, the frontier media began calling Ketchum "Black Jack," even after the mistake was corrected.

Regardless of how it happened, the name stuck. And the gang grew stronger and bolder.

New to the Cimarron area, the Ketchum brothers and their associates weren't identified as murderers and train robbers so they regularly appeared at dances, social functions, and saloons in and around town. They made friends easily and spent money with reckless abandon, so they became local favorites. Their popularity faded quickly, however, when their new friends discovered what they did for a living.

Then, in 1896, the Ketchums arrived in Liberty, a small settlement near Tucumcari, where they broke into a store and post office operated by Levi and Morris Herzstein and helped themselves to money and supplies. After discovering the break-in the next morning, Levi Herzstein and three friends—Merejildo Gallegos, Placido Gurule, and Atancio Borque—set out in pursuit. It was a mistake—a fatal mistake.

Tom and Sam spotted the riders headed toward them and opened fire, killing Herzstein and Gallegos and seriously wounding Gurule. While Borque was fleeing the scene, Tom Ketchum pumped bullets into the bodies of Herzstein and Gallegos until he emptied his rifle. Gurule, however, escaped Tom's wrath by pretending to be dead until the brothers rode off. Years later, he spotted Tom in a Las Vegas, New Mexico, railroad station and identified him as one of the men who had attacked the group. But no charges were ever filed despite Gurule's pleas for justice, an apparent testimony to the city's lax laws and dishonest lawmen.

In the meantime, it was business as usual for the Ketchum brothers and their gang. In May 1897, they stopped a Southern Pacific train in southwestern Texas and made off with forty-two thousand dollars. They returned to Cimarron and lived it up until they ran out of money. But before their next heist, the Ketchums decided they needed a hideout. They selected an isolated area in Turkey Canyon, about ten miles outside of Cimarron, where they constructed three crude wooden shacks. Then they went back to work.

That September, they held up a Colorado and Southern passenger train outside of Folsom and made off with an estimated fifteen thousand dollars. Over the next two years, the Ketchums were the principal suspects in seven more train robberies in Colorado and New Mexico.

But then, they began making mistakes.

Less than two years after relieving the Colorado and Southern train of its payroll, they decided to do it again. This time, however, only Sam and three other gang members—Will Carver, Bruce "Red" Weaver, and William "Elza" Lay—participated because Black Jack had left the gang after a dispute with his brother. Even without him, the robbery was a success and the bandits made off with more than twenty thousand dollars. But they also made mortal enemies.

One of them was Edward Farr, the sheriff of Huerfano County, Colorado. After hearing about the second Colorado and Southern robbery, Farr rode into New Mexico, teamed up with railroad agent W. H. Reno and five deputies, and went hunting outlaws. J. H. Morgan, one of the posse members, knew about the gang's hideout in Turkey Canyon and suggested they start there. A fierce shoot-out erupted when they arrived; Farr and deputies W. H. Love and Tom Smith were killed. Two of the other four lawmen were wounded by the outlaws, who were using smokeless powder and steel-jacketed bullets, the latest advances in weaponry.

Sam Ketchum was badly wounded but managed to escape. Lay, Weaver, and Carver got away uninjured; Sam's freedom was brief. The posse found him three days later at the home of a rancher and carried him back to Cimarron on a hastily made stretcher. He was transferred to the New Mexico Territorial Prison, where doctors tried to save his life, but in vain.

Aware that he was probably not going to survive, Sam Ketchum confessed to a lengthy list of crimes, including the deaths of Colonel Albert Fountain and his eight-year-old son, Henry. He said Fountain, a special investigator for the Southeastern New Mexico Stock Growers Association, was close to bringing indictments against the Ketchums for cattle rustling. He was ambushed and murdered, along with his son, when he refused to stop the court action. Sam said he pleaded with his brother to spare the boy, but Tom insisted he was a witness and therefore had to be killed.

The double murder had gone unsolved since it occurred on February 1, 1896. The Ketchum brothers were considered suspects, but so were several others because Albert Fountain had many enemies.

Fountain served in the Civil War as a Union soldier, then got a law degree and moved to Texas, where he was soon elected to the state legislature. He won two terms in the Senate, and at one time acted as lieutenant governor ex officio, filling a vacant post. However, his radical Republican views angered his rival Democrats so much that he was challenged to several duels. He killed an opponent during one of them.

In 1873, Fountain and his wife moved to Mesilla, New Mexico, where his law practice flourished. He was appointed assistant district attorney, probate judge, and deputy court clerk. He also founded the *Mesilla Valley Independent,* a newspaper printed in English and Spanish. However, he wasn't always successful. In 1881, he defended Billy the Kid during his trial for the murder of Sheriff William Brady but lost the case and the Kid was sentenced to death. Fountain then moved to Las Cruces and served as a prosecutor during federal land fraud trials. In 1888, after returning to Mesilla, Fountain was elected to the territorial legislature. He became speaker of the House but lost his seat two years later. He then became a special prosecutor for the New Mexico Livestock Association, and by 1894 he had successfully convicted twenty men for cattle rustling.

But with success came enemies.

Although warned that his life was in danger, Fountain rode to Lincoln to help prosecute a case against Oliver Lee, a well-known gunman, and to gather indictments against several others, including the Ketchum brothers. After his court appearance, he and his son climbed into his buckboard and headed toward their home in Mesilla. They never got there.

Authorities found tracks from his wagon near White Sands, about seventy miles north of Mesilla. They also found several

Sam Ketchum (pictured here) and his brother terrorized New Mexico Territory.
HERZSTEIN MEMORIAL MUSEUM, CLAYTON, NM

empty cartridge cases, a necktie, the son's bloody handkerchief, the father's legal papers, and two pools of blood. The bodies were missing; so were a blanket, a quilt, and Fountain's rifle. After following the tracks, they found the buckboard and team but never any trace of the victims.

The Ketchums were immediately placed on the list of suspects, but Lee and two of his associates, Jim Gilliland and William McNew, got the most attention from authorities. All three were eventually brought to trial for the murder of Henry Fountain; no one was ever charged with the father's death. All three were acquitted. Their attorney was Albert Fall, who had become one of Fountain's bitter rivals after losing the 1888 election to him. Since no bodies were ever found, the case remained open, even after Sam Ketchum's confession. Speculation continued that the three accused men had hired the Ketchums to commit the murders.

Sam Ketchum died of blood poisoning caused by the bullet wounds on July 24, 1899. He was forty-five years old.

And time was running out for Black Jack.

After leaving the gang, Tom moved to Arizona, where he murdered two men while holding up a store. With a posse on his trail, he slipped back into New Mexico. The news of his brother's death hadn't reached him when he decided to stage a train robbery by himself. And he chose the same train that Sam and the others had held up about a month before.

But things didn't go right.

He stopped the train on a curve, leaving it in a cramped position that made it impossible to uncouple the cars. Despite that, Black Jack continued with his plan. He got into the baggage car and shot a mail clerk. But then he ran into Frank Harrington, who had been the conductor on the two previous Ketchum-staged holdups. Tired of being a victim, Harrington had armed himself with a twelve-gauge shotgun. When the train stopped, he realized almost instantly what was happening and walked to the baggage car, opened the door, and pointed his shotgun at Ketchum. The outlaw spotted him first and got off one shot. It missed. Harrington cut loose with his twelve-gauge. The blast nearly tore Ketchum's right arm off, and he fell backward from the car. Harrington quickly ordered the engineer to power up the locomotive and pull the train away. They stopped at every station along the way to alert authorities of the robbery attempt and told them to look for a wounded man near the scene.

The next day, lawmen found Black Jack about one hundred yards from the scene, badly wounded and ready to surrender. He said he had tried to get on his horse and ride away, but the pain was too great so he sat down to wait for the inevitable. (Another version of the arrest says that early the next morning, he flagged down a passing freight train, but when it stopped, he pulled a gun on the crewmen who tried to help him. When they threatened to leave him there because of his unfriendly attitude, he said he was "all done in" and asked them to take him in. They fashioned a stretcher, put him in the caboose, and took him to Folsom, where deputies took over.)

He was rushed to Santa Fe, where prison doctors amputated what was left of his arm. Then he was jailed. Appeals followed; so did the denials. Almost two years later, April 6, 1901, arrived and Black Jack Ketchum was taking his final steps. After reaching the platform atop the scaffold, he gazed stoically at the crowd as a deputy placed the noose around his neck and a hood over his head. Sheriff Sergio Garcia cut the rope holding the trapdoor, and Black Jack Ketchum plunged to his death.

It was not a pleasant sight. The inexperienced executioners had miscalculated Ketchum's weight and the length of the drop. During a test run, they had attached bags of sand weighing about two hundred pounds to the rope and pushed it off the gallows. But that stretched the rope and made it thinner. Also, the noose was improperly tied so it slipped easily. As a result, when Ketchum plunged through the trapdoor, his head was ripped from his body as the rope tightened. Only the hood, which had been pinned to his shirt, prevented the head from rolling away.

Some spectators groaned; others turned away. The executioners rushed down from the gallows and lifted the body off the ground. Doctors pronounced him dead and then clumsily reattached the head. He was buried about an hour later in a grave on a nearby prairie that served as Clayton's Boot Hill.

A rumor quickly spread that the dead man was not Black Jack Ketchum. According to that theory, his older brother, Green, had bribed the sheriff with several horses to hang a man who had been dead for three days instead of Ketchum. That, so the story went, was the reason the head snapped off so easily. However, several photographs of a one-armed man standing on the gallows with a noose around his neck dispelled any such notion.

But the saga of Black Jack Ketchum didn't end there.

The body remained in the prairie grave until the 1930s, when some local historians figured the outlaw deserved a better final resting place. So, according to local newspaper clippings of the time, they dug up his wooden coffin while thousands of spectators gathered to watch the exhumation. Then they all followed the wagon to a new burial site in the community cemetery, where the body still rests. Today, a granite headstone denotes the grave, rather than the wooden marker that once stood over his remains.

In 1956, Columbia Pictures released *Blackjack Ketchum, Desperado,* a full-length movie in which Howard Duff portrayed Ketchum as a sort of antihero. Sam Ketchum wasn't even mentioned. It was not well received.

CHAPTER SIXTEEN

Christopher "Kit" Joy:
One of the Few Who Survived

The headline over a story published in the *Albuquerque Morning Journal* on March 11, 1884, blared: "Will Rob No More."
Underneath, the subhead trumpeted:
"The Whole Gang of Train Robbers Bite the Dust."
Below that, another subhead proclaimed:
"Mitch Lee, Kit Joy, Frank Taggart and Geo. Cleveland Gone Where the Woodbine Twineth and the Wicked Cease from Troubling."

The story was about a gang of train robbers. They broke out of a Silver City jail. They let two other prisoners come along. A posse formed and went after them. A desperate fight ensued. Posse member J. W. Lafferr, "one of our town's most estimable citizens," was killed. So were two of the escapees. Two others were captured. Both were hanged a half mile from where they were captured by "a party of determined citizens."

The story continued that Kit Joy, the escapee who allegedly shot and killed Lafferr, was still at large but added that "a party of three started in pursuit of Joy, and it is believed that he was overtaken and killed as his pursuers are very reticent about the matter. In any event, he is badly wounded and his escape is simply impossible … [but] death for the desperadoes is a fitting one and nobody in the Territory will regret the fact that they are gone, never to return. There seems to be no doubt, but what Kit Joy has gone beyond."

The report also noted that Lafferr was "esteemed by all who knew him and that he should meet his death at the hands of such a gang seems almost unbearable."

The newspaper's supposition about the death of Kit Joy was incorrect. He didn't go to That Big Corral Up in the Sky until fifty-two years later. And it was old age and illness that did him in, not a lawman's bullet or a hangman's noose.

Joy's tale was typical of the times. Essentially, he was a cowboy who didn't like toiling long hours for cowboy wages, so he formulated a get-rich-quick plan that didn't work out as planned. He got caught. Usually, that's the end of the story except for variations of the final paragraphs. Some were shot and killed; others were sent to prison. Joy was among those given lengthy sentences, but he survived and lived into his seventies.

It all started around 1860, when Christopher Joy was born in Texas. Sometime during his youth, he started using the nickname Kit and continued calling himself that until his latter years. The family moved to Hillsboro, New Mexico Territory, in the mid-1880s, and Kit spent some time in Tombstone, Arizona Territory, before returning to New Mexico and settling down in Silver City, where he found work on area ranches.

Silver City didn't offer much in the way of excitement that catered to the desires of the young, and sometimes reckless, cowpuncher. In his book, *Evolution of a Train Robber*, author Edgar Beecher Bronson observed, "Outside the towns, there were only three occupations in Grant County … cattle ranching, mining and fighting the Apache, all of a sort to attract and hold none but the sturdiest types of real manhood, men inured to danger and reckless of it. In the early eighties no faint-heart came to Grant County unless he blundered in—and any such were soon burning the shortest trail out."

Within the towns, Bronson continued, there were also only three ways to make a living—supplying the cowboys and miners with whatever they needed, gambling, and "figuring out how to slip through the next 24 hours without getting a heavier load of lead in one's system than could be conveniently carried."

Christopher Joy chose working on a cattle ranch, but he wanted more.

To ease the monotony of sitting on a horse and watching bovines for endless hours, Joy and his saddle mates frequently rode into Silver City on payday, got drunk, and shot out city lights. Or they taught tenderfoots the "cowboy's hornpipe," a spirited dance to the accompaniment of bullets splattering between their feet.

Back on the ranch, while spending lonely nights and dusty days riding herd, Joy began fantasizing about life in the big cities, particularly San Francisco. He dreamed about the women in their brightly colored dresses, of riding on trolley cars instead of well-worn saddles, and of the countless saloons lining both sides of every street. But the visions of grandeur quickly gave way to the harsh reality that he was never going to get there on the thirty-five dollars a month he earned herding cattle.

He needed a plan.

He also needed associates to help him carry it out.

History does not record which came first—the plan or the conspirators. Either way, he rolled the imaginary dice and the numbers came up—a gang of four and a train robbery.

By asking around, Joy found three cowpokes who were also fed up with steers, dust, sweat, and horses. Mitch Lee and Frank Taggart matched Joy in temperament; George Washington Cleveland was known as daring and willing to try anything. None of them needed much convincing.

Once the gang was in place, Joy selected the target—a Southern Pacific train that would make a stop at Gage Station, manned by a lone operator just west of Deming in Grant County. The quartet laid careful plans. They requested time off from their ranch duties and then rode off toward Silver City. They arrived separately, bought some provisions, and parted company again as they rode out of town. The met up again at a predetermined rendezvous along the Mimbres River. On November 24, 1883, they rode into Gage together and set their plan into action.

Faced with a battery of six-guns pointed directly at him, the station agent offered no resistance. Docile in the face of death, he obeyed without hesitation when Joy ordered him to stop the train. Theophilus C. Webster, the engineer, recognized the signal and applied the air brakes. The locomotive's iron wheels screeched against the tracks as the slowing process started, and the train had nearly come to a halt when it reached the station. But then Webster noticed that the agent was surrounded by armed bandits. He reacted instantly and pulled the throttle open in an attempt to power the engine up again. The effort was in vain. The outlaws realized he was trying to get away. Mitch Lee fired once. Webster fell dead.

No one else tried to avoid the unavoidable. Joy's gang began shouting and firing wildly to terrorize the remaining crew and passengers. The tactics worked; there were no further threats to the successful completion of their plan. For the next fifteen minutes, the bandits looted the express and postal cars, then turned their guns on the frightened passengers and made them surrender their money and jewels. With their mission accomplished, they rode off into the night, north toward the Mimbres River in the hope that the loose sand along the riverbank would cover their tracks.

They stashed their loot and nonchalantly returned to Silver City, where they planned to wait until the furor over the train robbery subsided. Then they would divide the loot and return to their day jobs. But the commotion didn't subside.

Alerted by telegraph, lawmen from Silver City, Deming, and Lordsburg were quick to arrive at the scene. Veteran Grant County Sheriff Harvey Whitehill organized a posse, and the search was on. For several days, the lawmen scoured the area without results. But then they came across an unlikely clue that helped them break the case. While riding the plains north of Gage, Whitehill discovered a scrap torn from a newspaper printed in a Kansas town. He remembered that a Silver City merchant was originally from that town, so he hustled back and questioned the man. He said that he was a subscriber and that he had wrapped the newspaper around some provisions sold to two men. He identified one of them as George Cleveland.

Two days later, Whitehill found Cleveland in Socorro. After making an arrest, he told Cleveland that all the other gang members were in custody and that they had fingered him as the engineer's murderer. It was a lie, but it worked. Threatened with a first-degree

Christopher "Kit" Joy rustled cattle and murdered people.
SCOTTSDALE CC SOUTHWEST STUDIES

murder charge, Cleveland didn't hesitate and gave up the names of the other three. Taggart was nabbed within a month; Joy and Lee stayed on the run a while longer, until greed and another lie helped bring them in.

Sheriff Whitehill was well known in the territory for a simple act performed years earlier—he was the first lawman to arrest Billy the Kid. In April 1875 he brought the fifteen-year-old into his jail on a charge of stealing butter. Whitehill said at the time that he didn't want to throw the boy behind bars, only to "scare some sense into him." He released him the next morning, then had to arrest him again the following September, this time for abetting the burglary of a laundry.

Whitehill, born in Ohio in 1837, moved to Leadville, Colorado, in 1859 and took up mining. He was one of the first prospectors to find gold and within a year, he dug a reported fifteen thousand dollars out of his claim. In the mid-1860s, he migrated to New Mexico Territory and worked as a freighter, miner, and mercenary, fighting in the Apache Wars. He was elected sheriff of Grant County in 1874 and moved into his new headquarters in Silver City, an extremely lawless community where, according to an early newspaper report, "death on the street here is an almost daily occurrence that we citizens are forced to meekly endure and tolerate because a popping firecracker sends our lawmen scurrying."

Shortly after taking office, Whitehill hired Dan Tucker, also known as "Dangerous Dan," as his chief deputy. Although Silver City residents violently disagreed with the choice because Tucker was a notorious gunman, the two worked well together and brought a degree of calm to the troubled city. It took numerous shoot-outs with outlaws, drunks, troublemakers, and rowdy miners, but the pair got the job done by court convictions, legal hangings, and a few executions that might have been slightly illegal, but were acceptable under the circumstances.

Whitehill served six terms as sheriff of the county and one term in the territorial legislature. His career as a lawman ended in 1891, when he was indicted for allowing a prisoner to escape. The charge was dropped, but since his days as a sheriff were over, he turned to farming and cattle ranching. He died in Deming in 1905.

Furious over the Gage robbery, the railroad and Wells Fargo were offering rewards totaling eight thousand dollars for the capture and conviction of the four robbers. The news brought the bounty hunters out in force, a factor that sent Lee and Joy into hiding. In late January 1884, line rider Charley Perry encountered two men who said they were looking for work. Perry suspected they might be the fugitives, so after telling them he had no jobs available and sending them on their way, he contacted Deputy Sheriff Andrew Best. Smart enough to realize that they probably couldn't take the outlaws by simply demanding that they surrender, Best and Perry decided to use trickery.

Over in Socorro, convicted murderer Joel Fowler was being threatened by an angry lynch mob. Without revealing their identities and purpose, the deputy and the cowhand caught up with the robbers and told them that if they would help spring Fowler from jail, they would be handsomely rewarded by his rich friends. Joy and Lee bought it. The newly organized quartet set out for Socorro, about 120 miles away. On the first night of their journey, and unaware that they were being duped, Joy and Lee fell asleep as they sat around the campfire. Their new companions quickly disarmed them and made the arrests. They took their prisoners into Socorro and put them in the local jail for safekeeping until they could be transferred to Silver City. Joel Fowler was in the same jail. Two nights later, the mob broke down the door, dragged Fowler into the street, and lynched him. Joy and Lee cowered in their cells as they watched it happen.

The two were eventually returned to Silver City and thrown into the jail that was already the temporary home of Cleveland and Taggart. But it was a brief stay. Overwhelmed with the fear that Fowler's fate might also befall them, the four overpowered their guard and escaped, taking fellow prisoners Carlos Chavez and Charles Spencer with them. They stole horses and raced out of town. The posse formed quickly and overtook the escapees six miles north of town. In the ensuing gun battle, Lafferr, Cleveland, and Chavez were killed. Lee and Taggart were captured and hanged on the spot. A newspaper reporter noted that Lee was weak from loss of blood and died almost immediately, but Taggart "died of hard strangulation, a throat disease that is extremely common among his ilk in this section." Spencer was allowed to live after he showed posse members that his gun had not been fired. He was returned to jail. Despite what the newspaper story surmised, Kit Joy got away.

Once again, however, his freedom was short-lived.

He managed to make his way to the northern portion of Grant County, surviving by traveling at night and stealing food. But local ranchers, spurred by the threat of a train robber pilfering their belongings and by visions of sharing the reward money, organized a non-deputized posse and set out to capture him. On March 21, 1884, the searchers spotted their quarry. One of them, Erichus "Rackety" Smith, opened fire. His first shot missed; the second hit Joy in the leg, just below the knee. Unable to resist, Joy surrendered and was taken back to Silver City, where his leg was amputated. When he was able to stand trial, Joy was convicted of second-degree murder for his involvement in the death of the railroad engineer, but he was never charged in Lafferr's death. Stephen F. Wilson, the newly appointed judge of the Second Judicial District, sentenced Joy to life in prison. Kit Joy's brief foray into the criminal world was over.

As Joy was getting ready for his trial, a furor erupted over the disbursement of the eight thousand dollars in reward money. There were many claimants. Lawmen, bounty hunters, posse members, attorneys, and vigilantes all demanded their share. A judge finally divided the pot, dispensing payments ranging from $1,333.33 to $444.44 to settle the arguments.

But nobody ever recovered the loot from the train robbery.

While imprisoned, Joy learned the tailor's trade and eventually became the penitentiary's chief tailor. In 1889, his sentence was commuted from life to twenty years. In 1891, his attorney appealed for a full pardon, but E. C. Wade, the prosecutor at Joy's trial, issued a strenuous objection. In a letter to Governor L. Brad-ford Prince, Wade contended that the accused "belongs to the 'Dime Novel' order of young desperadoes ... wanting in all moral sense and would be, but for the loss of his leg, a most dangerous man."

Four years later, after serving only twelve years, he was released by Colonel E. H. Bergman, the prison superintendent, who certified that, coupled with good behavior, the terms of the original sentence had been fulfilled. Acting governor Lorian Miller issued a pardon and restored Joy's citizenship. This upset some of his contemporaries, particularly Donald Kedzie, editor of the *Lordsburg Western Liberal,* who editorialized:

> *It is reported that [Joy] is dying of consumption. It is just as well to let a cold-blooded murderer like Joy die in a penitentiary as outside, and it is a better plan to have the sheriff strangle them before they are sent to the peniten-tiary than to run the risk of their contracting an incurable disease while confined in that territorial institution.*

After his release, Joy went to live with his mother in Kings-ton. They moved to Fort Huachuca, Arizona Territory, in 1900, and he opened a tailor shop, using the skills he learned while incar-cerated. After his mother's death in 1911, he moved his shop to nearby Buena. Business was good for a while. The US Army had mobilized forces to chase Mexican bandit Pancho Villa into Mex-ico after his raid on Columbus, New Mexico, on March 9, 1916. The pursuit route went along the Lewis Springs–Fort Huachuca railroad spur near Joy's shop. The troopers needed uniforms, pro-ducing a demand for Joy's tailoring expertise. But the good times didn't last. The need for army uniforms declined after World War I; Buena dried up and became a ghost town shortly afterward.

Handicapped by old age and his physical condition, Joy had to close his business and move to nearby Garden Canyon. Things got worse, and he found it almost impossible to make a decent living. So the one-legged tailor, just like the daydreaming cowboy, fell victim to the lure of ill-gotten riches. During the early years of Prohibition, Joy hooked up with Warren Mimms and they went into the liquor business. Their modus operandi involved importing whiskey and wine from Mexico, brewing up some of their own special brand of moonshine, and selling it to those who thirsted in the Huachuca Mountains.

That venture didn't work out well, either. In May 1926, the two were arrested by federal agents and charged with violations of the National Prohibition Act. They appeared before District Court Judge William Sawtelle in Tucson; both entered guilty pleas. Sawtelle fined them a dollar each on two charges and sentenced them to jail time.

Released after serving five months, Joy went back to Garden Canyon. Ten years later, at the age of seventy-six, he entered the Cochise County hospital in Douglas, suffering from pneumonia and influenza. He died there on April 14, 1936. His death went virtually unnoticed.

CHAPTER SEVENTEEN

George Musgrave:
A Respectable Murderer

The scenario might someday become part of a twenty-first-century western movie. It's a true story, and it reflects the lawlessness that plagued New Mexico from the mid-1800s until the turn of the century. It unfolded like this:

On October 19, 1896, two cowboys rode into a roundup camp on a range southwest of Roswell and were welcomed with a customary "Howdy, stranger." They weren't shifty-eyed. They didn't have notches on their six-guns. They were both young, maybe in their late teens or early twenties. Their names were George Musgrave and Bob Hayes, but nobody asked. They would have given fake identities anyway.

It was close to noon, so the roundup crew invited the newcomers over to the chuck wagon for the usual range grub of bacon, cold sourdough biscuits, and the omnipresent beans. The cook, Sam Butler, was a little suspicious. Strangers were often outlaws, and outlaws were running roughshod all across New Mexico Territory.

However, nobody said anything. Cowpunchers weren't normal robbery targets; their wages were a paltry thirty dollars a month, and they usually spent most of that on one Saturday night after payday, so they didn't have much worth stealing. The strangers finished lunch, returned the tin plates and flatware to the chuck wagon, and engaged in small talk.

Then George Parker rode in. He was an ex–Texas Ranger who was ramrodding the cattle drive. He recognized Musgrave. They had once worked together, so he approached him with an extended hand. Musgrave stood up, faked a smile, and pretended to accept the greeting. But when they got within handshaking distance of each other, Musgrave drew his pistol and fired four times. All four bullets hit the unsuspecting Parker, and he fell to the ground mortally wounded. Because the two were so close together when the shots were fired, Parker's clothing burst into flames.

The stunned cowhands had no time to react before Hayes hauled out his six-gun and ordered them to remain calm. This was a personal matter and none of their business, he said. Musgrave stood over the smoldering body and warned the others that he'd kill the first man to make a move. "I don't want to hurt any of you boys," he muttered, "but I came a long way to kill this son-of-a-bitch [because] he caused me a lot of trouble." Musgrave said the dead man had turned him into the law when the two were partners.

The partnership was illegal from the very beginning. Four months after his seventeenth birthday, Musgrave and Parker hatched a moneymaking scheme that involved rustled cattle and stolen horses. Parker and his associate, Ernest Bloom, illegally removed the horses and altered their brands while Musgrave pilfered at least six head of cattle. According to the plan, the horse thieves would trade their goods to Musgrave for his cattle, plus some cash. The young rustler held up his part of the deal and delivered the cows. But he received nothing in return because another of Parker's associates, C. D. Bonney, had stolen the stolen horses. They were his in the first place; he was in on the plot.

Once he had the cattle, Parker warned Musgrave to leave the territory because there was going to be trouble. Musgrave took his advice and left. But while he was away, Parker went to Musgrave's parents' ranch and confiscated all his mother's cattle, telling her that her son had stolen them. And when a grand jury later indicted Musgrave for cattle rustling, Parker testified against him. Musgrave never faced the charges. Instead, he became a fugitive on a full-time basis.

But he never forgot. And now, two years later, he had evened the score.

The young killer and his partner then stole two fresh horses and saddles and rode off toward Bootheel country in the southwestern corner of New Mexico. Posses formed to give chase, but that was nothing new to Musgrave. He had spent most of his time over the past few months eluding lawmen, almost from the day he joined with the High Fives.

He was only seventeen years old when he developed a bad case of wanderlust that prompted him to move from his native Texas to New Mexico. His family, headed by father Bennett Musgrave, did well as ranchers and had a fairly comfortable lifestyle in Atascosa County, Texas, where George was born in 1877, the last of five children. He worked on the ranch until 1894, when he migrated west to New Mexico and found work on other ranches, including one where his brother, Calvin (also known as Van), had been promoted to ranch foreman. He spent most of his spare time with Code Young, a twenty-five-year-old cattle rustler. They had come to New Mexico together and shortly after their arrival, they hooked up with Hayes, another fugitive from Texas justice. That association led to other jobs raising cows in New Mexico and Arizona. It also brought them into contact with the Christian brothers, Bob and Will, more commonly known as Black Jack. And that relationship led directly to steady employment in the fields of bank robbing, stagecoach holdups and, eventually, murder.

They formed the High Fives, named after a card game popular at the time. Four of the members were cut from the same cloth— hardened Texas cowboys who held no respect for the law and who didn't like working hard for their money. But Musgrave didn't quite fit the mold. He was soft-spoken, cheerful, handsome, and had good table manners. He dressed well, impressed the ladies with his quick wit, and had a magnetic personality that was later considered the reason for his acceptance into the gang.

Musgrave was only nineteen when the gang staged its first robbery, only a few months before his deadly encounter with the former Ranger. The outlaw quintet rode into Separ and pulled up in front of the general store that also housed the post office. Two of them stayed outside to hold the horses; Musgrave, Young, and Black Jack entered with guns drawn and demanded cash, coin, and anything else they considered useful, including blankets, cigars, whiskey, tack, gloves, and small weapons. Their monetary take was slightly more than two hundred dollars, not much for a five-way split. Even worse, their victims had recognized some of them.

The crime was reported, but not much happened. Grant County Sheriff Baylor Shannon didn't appear to be too interested in mounting up and riding out, because he waited two days before sending a couple of deputies out on the already-cold trail. They tracked the robbers into Arizona, but the High Fives had slipped across the Mexican border. Then they came back into Arizona and tried to hold up a Nogales bank on August 6, 1896. The attempt was a total failure. Bank employees, confronted by Musgrave's two pistols, panicked and ran out a back door to raise the alarm. The cashier, however, stayed behind and countered Musgrave's threat by firing his own six-shooter. Nobody got hurt, but the bandits knew better than to stick around because the citizens were taking up arms and coming after them. They escaped in a hail of gunfire. The effort had been for nothing. Even worse, two of their horses were killed as they fled.

Now there was no safe place to hide. The High Fives were wanted almost everywhere they went, so they separated. Musgrave and Black Jack rode to the border town of Bowie in southeastern Arizona. Bob Christian, Young, and Hayes were tracked to Skeleton Canyon on the Arizona–New Mexico border, where they killed Frank Robson, a US Customs agent, during a gun battle. All three escaped into New Mexico's Animas Valley and then brazenly rode into Deming to stock up on supplies. Once the residents there realized who the visitors were, they armed themselves and prepared for a battle. But the trio left without making any effort to relieve the locals of any belongings.

Meanwhile, Musgrave and Black Jack weren't doing much better. They robbed a store in Bowie but netted only two pair of boots. The store owner later revealed that they had missed more than thirteen hundred dollars he kept in a sack of coffee.

Things were also taking a turn for the worse on the legal front. A US District Court in Silver City returned indictments for all five High Fives for robbing the post office at Separ, a federal violation. The legal action didn't impress the gang members because they were veteran fugitives from the law. But bad luck made earning a living their way extremely difficult. They had failed miserably in their last two robbery attempts, and the store holdups had profited them very little. Rather than quit the profession, however, they adapted. They would try their luck as train and stagecoach robbers.

That didn't work out well, either. Not at first, anyway.

On the night of October 2, 1896, the gang attempted to stop and rob the Atlantic and Pacific train at a crossing over the Rio Puerco, about thirty-five miles southwest of Albuquerque. As the train slowly made its way up a small hill, Musgrave and two others jumped aboard and ordered the engineer to make an unscheduled stop. Then one of them fired two shots at a brakeman, and that alerted the passengers. Unfortunately for the High Fives, one of the passengers was Will Loomis, a deputy US marshal who was returning from serving a subpoena in Gallup. He had been chasing the gang for more than two months. After hearing the shots, he hoisted his shotgun out of the seat next to him and slipped from the train. As his eyes adjusted to the darkness, Loomis spotted Code Young and fired. Although hit, Young was able to get off two shots in the lawman's direction. But a second shotgun blast ended the confrontation. Young crawled toward his partners, screaming that he had been shot and was, in his words, "done for." But they didn't hear his cries and, realizing that the robbery attempt had been thwarted, rode away.

Once again, the posse formed. Once again, it came up empty. The remaining gang members headed east; the posse, which hadn't formed until six hours after the robbery attempt, scoured the southwest.

Young's body was taken to Albuquerque, where it was photographed, then buried in a public cemetery.

Although dealing with a string of defeats, the High Fives (now the High Fours) weren't about to quit. But they did change their strategy. Next time, a stagecoach would be the target.

Five days after the train debacle, they targeted the eastbound San Antonio-to-White Oaks stage line, which had never been held up in its sixteen years of operation. The gang put an end to that record and scored what, for them, was a major success. The First National Bank of Las Vegas had entrusted a five-hundred-dollar shipment to the stage line; the outlaws got all of it. They also took the driver's hat, boots, and horses, forcing him to walk barefoot eight miles back to the station to report the incident.

Now flushed with success, the quartet rode into a stage station about thirty miles west of White Oaks. They ordered food, ate it, and then robbed the stationmaster of $6.50. Encouraged by the five-hundred-dollar haul from the first stage robbery, they held up the westbound stage less than six hours later, but Lady Luck again deserted them. They tore open mail sacks but came up with only about thirty-two dollars. Frustrated, they also took the driver's tobacco and knife and a passenger's hat, gloves, and pipe. When the passenger pleaded that he was a poor working man, they gave him seven dollars from their loot.

Apparently, the robbers considered themselves "good ol' boys," rather than criminals. On several occasions, they ordered their victims to drink whiskey with them. At least twice, they marched their victims, at gunpoint, down the town's main street and then toasted them with stolen booze before riding off into the night.

The frustrated lawmen continued the chase, even after it led to disaster. While camped near Squaw Mountain in eastern Arizona, members of a posse accidentally shot and killed one of their own, Frank Galloway, when they mistook him for a gang member. The High Fives (or Fours) managed to stay out of sight, but it was getting more difficult. The Southern Pacific Railroad donated an engine and a freight car, which made it easier for the sheriffs, marshals, and deputies to travel cross-country with their horses in their relentless pursuit. The railroads also contributed to the reward fund, now at a thousand dollars for each criminal. That, coupled with persistence and determination, finally resulted in an ambush of the foursome.

After loading their horses into the freight car at Deming, the lawmen correctly figured that the outlaws were headed toward a well-known camp. They got there first and positioned themselves in and around a small camp structure. Then they waited. It was November 18, 1896.

As dawn broke, four riders approached, cautiously working their way to the campground. There were lawmen on their trail, but they were hungry and the thought of a hearty breakfast allayed their fear of being captured. They rode on in. The lawmen recognized them as George Musgrave, Bob Hayes, and the Christian brothers. As they neared the ambush site, a ranch hand waved his hat from the corral in an apparent attempt to warn the outlaws. But they mistook it for a sign of welcome and rode forward. A deputy quickly stood up and ordered them to surrender. When they refused, the gunfire erupted.

Bob Hayes was the first to go down after taking bullets in the leg and foot. He fell to the ground and started shooting. His revolver was down to its last bullet when Hayes took a fatal shot to the forehead.

Black Jack Christian's horse was also hit, and the injured animal started bucking, wrenching his rider's six-gun from his hand. As the horse fell, Christian grabbed his rifle and began firing. Under the cover of all the gun smoke, he worked his way to safety in a nearby arroyo. He crawled through the arroyo to the top of a ridge and hid there until the lawmen left. Bob Christian and Musgrave, still on their horses, didn't stick around long enough to see what happened next. When the shooting died down, the only casualty was Hayes.

Although down to three charter members, the High Fives still hadn't learned that crime was not a profitable undertaking. No longer a high-level outfit, they nonetheless continued their banditry. Musgrave's brother Van and others signed on as temporary replacements for Hayes and Young, and the spree continued. They robbed a combination general store and post office in Cliff of slightly more than two hundred dollars. They also took such items as jewelry, underwear, boots, scarf pins, tobacco, knives, and a pistol. Then they ordered the store owner and his clerk to join them in the local saloon, where they were forced to down large amounts of whiskey. As a final gesture, the bandits appropriated two horses from the stage line and rode out of town.

They were able to elude the law because New Mexico was sparsely populated, the Mexican border was rarely more than a one-day ride away, and gang members were regarded as sort of folk heroes by the locals, who blamed government policies and banks for many of their tribulations. While the bandits were often courteous and kind, lawmen and posse members were considered hard-drinking, crude men who would "spit tobacco juice all over the floor."

Two weeks after the robbery at Cliff, Black Jack and one of his new associates, Sid Moore, rode into a ranch near Silver City. The ranch owner invited them in for a meal. After they finished eating, the two shot and killed the owner and seriously wounded his cook for no apparent reason. Less than six months later, Black Jack was dead. Acting on an informant's tip, a posse cornered him in Cole Creek Canyon, across the border in Arizona, on April 27, 1897. He was mortally wounded in the gunfight, and membership in the once-feared High Fives dropped to two: Bob Christian and George Musgrave. Aware that the reward money being offered for their capture or death was growing, and that more seasoned and tougher lawmen were now on their trail, they stayed in hiding for longer periods. But they successfully held up a train near Grants and got away with an estimated ninety thousand dollars. Then they made their way into Mexico. The robbery so incensed the federal government that President William McKinley signed a warrant for the arrest and extradition of George Musgrave, Bob Christian, Code Young, and Robert Hayes, even though the latter two were dead. The warrant was never served. Musgrave and Christian fled to the Mexican border town of Fronteras, Sonora. Within weeks, they were arrested after a shooting spree. They were fined and released. Bob Christian disappeared into the pages of history, but Musgrave's saga was far from over.

He returned to the United States and wandered across the Southwest for while. He was spotted in Texas, Wyoming, and Arizona, working on ranches and railroads and as a saloon keeper. Then he fell in love with Jeanette "Jano" Magor, the orphaned daughter of a prominent Wyoming rancher. They wed in Denver on November 2, 1908, and moved to Grand Junction, Colorado, where George (using the alias of Robert Cameron) became a respected cattleman and president of the local Elks lodge.

Although more than a decade had passed since President McKinley's warrant had been issued, Musgrave was still a wanted man. After being recognized in Grand Junction, he sent his wife back to Wyoming and left on a "business trip" to Nebraska. But there, his luck ran out. Musgrave was arrested in North Platte, Nebraska, and was returned to Roswell to stand trial for the murder of George Parker.

Once the proceedings began, Musgrave relied on his boyish face and good looks to sway the jury. He brought his wife and infant son into the courtroom, a move that helped him assume the guise of an honest man. One newspaper account said he "looked more like a senator than a cattle rustler."

The model citizen ploy worked, and the jury acquitted Musgrave on the grounds that Parker, the victim, had allegedly drawn first. The jury took only thirty minutes to reach its verdict. Afterward, one Roswell citizen commented, "If I'd been on that jury, I'd [have] given George Musgrave a medal." Musgrave later related his version of Parker's death during an interview with a local newspaper. He claimed that Parker had threatened to kill him and "only when Parker dismounted and reached for his six-shooters ... I shot him." Musgrave left town in a hurry and returned to Texas. A newspaper report said he robbed a train on the way.

Whether or not that was true (he did brag about it in his later years), Musgrave made his final move. He changed his name to Robert Stewart, migrated to Paraguay, South America, and earned a reputation as a legendary "cattle dealer" who was "very well known in all circles," a probable inference that he returned to rustling in the Southern Hemisphere.

It was an up-and-down ride from then on. He organized gangs of rustlers and smuggled stolen cattle across the Paraguayan borders into Argentina and Brazil. He became rich and bought a large home in Asunción, using much of his wealth to pay off customs officials. His wife bore him a daughter. At one point, he opened a fake medical practice in Buenos Aires, Argentina, and bought a large boat, which became a major party site for his cronies. He also began consorting with women other than Jano, his wife.

She grew tired of it. Although she had undoubtedly been aware of, and even participated in, his illegal activities, she returned to the United States where her sister-in-law advised her to get a divorce. She returned to their second home in Buenos Aires, filed for divorce, and returned to her Wyoming home, leaving her two children with Musgrave. They later distanced themselves from their father and returned to the States. As a result, Musgrave began drinking heavily, alternately going on weeklong binges and then sobering up before hitting the bottle again.

Badly in need of something to straighten his life out, he returned to rustling. Relying on the skills learned during his time in New Mexico, Musgrave was soon "the most famous of gringo cattle-rustlers in South America." During that time, he once got the owner of a large ranch so drunk that he was able to sell him the same herd of five hundred cattle six times.

Still a ladies' man, Musgrave took a common-law wife who bore him a son and a daughter. But she also grew tired of his constant womanizing, shot him in the foot, and left with her children. Cattle rustling had lost its appeal as a source of income, so Musgrave turned to other pursuits, including smuggling, counterfeiting, and assassination. He was accused, but never charged, with being the brains behind the murder, or attempted murder, of several influential men in Argentina and Brazil. After a payroll messenger was mugged and robbed in Argentina, Musgrave was arrested for the last time. He posted bail, then was deported to Paraguay.

He was sixty-three years old and persona non grata in Brazil and Argentina. But Paraguay remained open to his talents. He married again and fathered three more children. But his health was rapidly failing due to throat cancer, and his days as a criminal were over.

He died on August 15, 1947, at age seventy in the home of Asunción's mayor. Funeral services were held the next day in both Protestant and Catholic churches. His wife and children didn't attend either service; only the wife of a longtime friend and the American consul were there. Rebel forces and government troops were fighting for control of Asunción at the time of his burial. As a result, bullets were splattering all around the cemetery when Musgrave was interred, a fitting end for a bandit who plied his trade on two continents.

CHAPTER EIGHTEEN

Bad Baca Boys:
How a Fine Old Name Earned Respect

One factor that made the latter years of the nineteenth century notable in the history of the New Mexico Territory was the high crime rate. Cattle rustling was so common that it almost became an acceptable profession. Bank clerks and stagecoach drivers, fearful of being held up, carried shotguns and sidearms. And violent death was a front-page topic in the frontier press almost every day.

During those years of lawlessness and terror, anyone named Baca was a frequent suspect due to the high incidence of crimes committed by men bearing the surname. This was unfortunate because the name has noble origins.

There are two versions of how the name emerged. According to one story, it is a variation of "Cabeza de Vaca" ("head of the cow"), a title bestowed upon Spanish shepherd Martin Alhaja by King Alfonso VIII of Castile. The lowly shepherd's placement of a cow skull on a vital road as a marker was said to be instrumental in the victory of the Spanish over the Moors during a crucial battle in Andalusia. Alhaja's reward included a coat of arms with cow skulls in its design.

The other possibility is that Fernan Ruiz, a Spanish knight, led his troops to a victory over the Moors at Córdoba in 1235. To honor his heroism, King Alfonso added "Cabeza de Vaca" to Ruiz's name. The custom reflected the area where the knight was born.

Despite such an honorable background, however, the list of bad Bacas in New Mexico was lengthy.

Abran Baca and two of his brothers murdered newspaper publisher Anthony Conklin in Socorro in 1880. Antonio Baca, the sec-

Socorro's Elfego I

Six-gui

Ca

by Micl

Elfego Baca was a minor outlaw who later became a hero.

ond brother, was captured a short time afterward but was shot and killed by authorities while trying to escape from jail.

Onofre Baca, the third brother, was arrested and brought to trial but was acquitted. The verdict proved to be fatal to his brother, Abran, however. An angry mob, furious at the jury's decision, stormed the jail where Abran was being held, forcibly removed him, and hanged him.

The lynch mob considered itself respectable in a twisted sort of way. It was formed under the leadership of Colonel Ethan Eaton, one of Conklin's closest friends, who believed the local justice system was not willing to bring the newspaperman's killers to trial. Conklin had been shot while leaving church on Christmas Eve, and several witnesses identified the Baca brothers as the assailants. However, lawmen of Hispanic descent had a reputation of putting family ties ahead of justice, and the constable in charge of the case, Juan Maria Garcia, was a close relative of the accused trio.

When Garcia refused repeated requests to charge the brothers, Eaton called for a series of meetings in the Socorro area and demanded that the residents themselves take care of the particular situation while restoring law and order to the community in general. The upshot of the meetings came on January 1, 1881, when a notice in the *Socorro Sun* announced that anyone deemed and designated as a lawbreaker would meet swift justice at the hands of the newly formed organization. By this time, the group had adopted the high-sounding name, "Committee of Safety." It was, however, nothing more than a vigilante outfit.

Eaton was very persuasive. Shortly after the announcement, almost every Anglo businessman in Socorro was pressured into joining the committee, which, though not a legal entity, began taking the law into its own hands. Eaton ran the organization with an iron grip, keeping a diary of suspected criminals and ordering action if law officials acted too slowly. Abran Baca became one of the first victims of the Committee of Safety.

But Hispanics weren't the only ones persecuted and executed. The committee also strung up Tom Gordon for killing the town marshal, then lynched Joel Fowler for the murder of a friend in a saloon fight. It was the last vigilante action in Socorro.

Besides the brothers, other Bacas contributed to the shame associated with the family name.

Patricio Baca was considered one of the most notorious horse thieves in the territory until he was killed in Chimayo in 1875.

José Baca spent a considerable portion of his adult life behind bars. An outlaw with a lengthy rap sheet, he was sent to prison in 1906 for the fifth time.

Celso Baca beat José de la Cruz Sandoval to death in Santa Rosa in 1884.

Cruz Baca, an outlaw and murderer, killed a Hillsboro man, W. H. Allen, in 1887.

Manuel Baca, perhaps the most notorious of all, acted as the judge for the bloodthirsty White Caps gang in Las Vegas in the 1890s. His duties included ordering the execution of disloyal gang members.

But then, along came Elfego Baca to save the family name. Or, at least, remove some of the stain—in a roundabout fashion.

Elfego Baca was not a hero. He was more of a rogue, a sort of antihero. Like so many others, he worked both sides of the law. He engineered two jailbreaks, had a price put on his head by Pancho Villa, and served as a mayor and sheriff. Even the incident that made him an authentic New Mexican legend had some questionable details.

His life started one February afternoon in 1865 during an outdoor athletic event in Socorro. His pregnant mother was playing a game similar to softball, and when she reached up to catch a ball, Elfego made an unexpected appearance, right there on the field. Both recovered and accompanied the rest of the family on a planned trip to Topeka, Kansas. But a group of nomadic Indians attacked their wagon near Albuquerque, and one-year-old Elfego was taken captive. Surprisingly, the baby was returned to his parents four days later, and the trip to Kansas resumed. Later, when he achieved legendary status, folks claimed that even then, he was too much to handle.

The family stayed in Topeka for eight years, until the mother died in 1872. Elfego was shipped back to Socorro to work on a ranch owned by a relative. A year later, his father returned to New Mexico and became the sheriff in Belen, where he shot and killed two disorderly cowboys as part of his lawman's duties. Elfego was still working on the ranch, but when he heard that his father had been arrested, he walked from Socorro to the trial site in Los Lunas. He hid outside the jail until dark. When the lone guard left his post and joined some nearby festivities, Elfego used a ladder to break into the second story of the building, sawed a hole through the floor, reached down into the cell below, and hoisted his father to freedom. The elder Baca headed for Isleta, south of Albuquerque; Elfego returned to Socorro.

According to an oral biography he dictated in his later years, Elfego also met Billy the Kid during a roundup on the Ojo de Parida Ranch north of Socorro. Young and impetuous, the new friends made their way to Albuquerque for a night on the new railroad town that featured forty saloons. As they bar-hopped their way across the city's Old Town, they found ample amounts of liquor and women, but Billy complained that the surroundings were too quiet for his tastes. So, according to Baca, he decided to liven it up by firing a small gun he kept hidden under his derby hat.

"He [Billy] fired a shot [and] it made an awful noise," Baca recalled. "Here comes the deputy sheriff [who] searched both of us and was very mad." Unable to find the gun, the deputy left the scene, but when he got about a block away, Billy fired two more shots. The deputy ran back, searched both of them again, and threatened to arrest them for disturbing the peace. But he had to leave, angry and empty-handed, because it never occurred to him to look under the Kid's derby during his search for the gun.

However, the event that actually converted a carefree young cowhand into a folk legend took place over three days in October 1884.

At that time, violence was a way of life in San Francisco, a small town about 120 miles southwest of Socorro, better known by its shortened name of Frisco. Mexican-Americans had established a string of villages along the San Francisco River and named them the Upper, Lower, and Middle San Francisco Plazas. When Anglo settlers began showing up in the late 1870s, they renamed the Upper Frisco Plaza "Milligan's Plaza" after a merchant and saloon keeper. It would be the site of Elfego Baca's legend-making confrontation.

Elfego was working as a store clerk in Socorro when Pedro Sarracino, the deputy sheriff of Frisco, rode into town looking for deputies to help him control the drunken cowboys who were terrorizing his community. They all worked on the WS Ranch, named after its two founders, Montague Stevens and Harold Wilson, and managed by William French. Sarracino told Elfego how the ranch hands had tortured a Hispanic man who had a deformed back by pinning him to the floor, sitting on his arms and legs, and pounding on his chest to "straighten out his spine." His story inflamed young Baca. He chastised Sarracino for his reluctance to handle the situation by himself and was told that the job "was available to anyone who wants it." Without any official permission, Baca strapped on his six-shooter, pinned a kid's tin star on his chest, and rode 120 miles to Frisco as an unofficial deputy.

After arriving in Frisco, and despite having no legal powers, Elfego arrested Charles McCarty, a cowboy, on a charge of disorderly conduct. McCarty escaped, but Baca rode to the ranch where he worked and arrested him again, still without any real authority. About thirty other ranch hands observed the apprehension but made no move to interfere. Baca took the suspect back to Sarracino's house in Frisco and waited for the deputy to return from Socorro. Shortly afterward, a group of cowboys from the ranch rode up to the house and demanded their comrade's release. Baca refused, counted to three, and began firing. One of his bullets killed ranch foreman Young Parham's horse, and the rider died when it rolled on top of him.

The cowboys left, but two of them reappeared the next morning and offered to take the prisoner to jail in Frisco. Baca refused, even when the cowboys threatened that hundreds of men would be gunning for him if he insisted on keeping their saddle pard in custody. Baca stood firm, and the cowboys left again. Aware that trouble was brewing, Baca ordered the residents into a nearby church and then waited. When the cowboys returned with a small army, Baca walked directly into the group and disarmed two of them. But then, faced with overwhelming odds, Baca agreed to a compromise: He would free his prisoner after a hasty trial, but only if the cowboys would promise not to bother him when he left town. He also made them put it in writing. The mock trial was staged; the cowboy was fined five dollars and released. But when Baca refused to return McCarty's pistol, the big trouble started.

The vengeance-minded cowboys, already upset with Baca's arrogance and brashness, got uglier and surlier. Aware that he would be facing the mob all by himself, Baca backed out of the saloon that had served as a temporary courtroom and jumped into a jacal, a low one-room building made of cedar posts stuck into the ground and coated with adobe mud. He ordered the inhabitants to remove themselves, and the jacal became his refuge for the next thirty-six hours.

An estimated eighty cowboys had galloped into town, and now they surrounded the jacal. Angry because the unduly sworn lawman had humiliated them, they took up positions around the mud hut and began shooting rounds from every angle. Every bullet hit the jacal, but not one found its intended target. When cowpuncher Jim Hearne kicked the door open, he took a fatal slug to the belly and staggered back outside. The other cowboys responded with even more gunfire, but the walls of the jacal were thick enough to withstand the volleys.

Around sunset, one attacker lit a kerosene-soaked rag and threw it onto the roof of the jacal. The roof was sod so it didn't become fully engulfed, but part of it did catch fire and cause a partial collapse, apparently trapping the hapless self-appointed lawman. The cowboys called for a cease-fire, assuming that Baca would perish in the blaze. They waited until the next morning and then went to the jacal to retrieve the body. But their anticipation turned to mortification when they saw that their intended target had not only survived, but also was cooking breakfast. To further infuriate the mob, Baca attached a statue of a saint to his hat and waved it back and forth behind one of the jacal's tiny openings. The cowboys immediately resumed the attack, but not one of their bullets hit either Baca or the icon.

The battle was in its second day when Sarracino, the real deputy sheriff, returned from Socorro and negotiated a truce that would let Baca leave the jacal. While the horde of cowboys watched, he surrendered to the deputy, but only after the lawman said he could keep his own gun and the pistol he had taken from McCarty. The number of rifle and pistol rounds he escaped was never definitely established. The immediate count was around three hundred; the figure reached as high as four thousand as the legend grew. There was also some dispute about the casualties. Baca later claimed that he had killed four cowboys and wounded eight more. But local historians said the death toll was only two—Hearne and Parham, the cowboy whose horse had crushed him.

Regardless of the numbers, Baca was arrested on the spot and ordered back to Socorro. With his guns still strapped to his side, Baca and the deputy traveled in a buckboard while several cowboys rode thirty feet behind. According to several historical accounts, two groups had planned to ambush the buckboard and dispose of Baca, but their attempts failed because each gang thought the other had taken care of the dirty business.

Once the entourage arrived in Socorro, Baca was charged with murder and placed in jail. He spent four months behind bars until he was brought to trial in Albuquerque. The bullet-riddled door of the jacal was removed and introduced as evidence by his attorneys. So was a broom with eight bullet scars in its handle. The ranch owners defended their employees and testified that the incident was "all in good fun." French, the ranch manager, later wrote about the shoot-out in *Some Recollections of a Western Ranchman: New Mexico 1883–1899*. He claimed that since most of the cowboys were from Texas, they "remembered the Alamo" and therefore had a longstanding grudge against Mexicans. "Under the influence of patriotism and whiskey, they proceeded to give vent to their feelings," he recalled.

Baca was quickly exonerated on the grounds of self-defense. He was ordered to stand trial a second time on another charge associated with the lengthy gunfight but was again acquitted.

Back in his hometown, Baca's popularity was at its peak. He was elected county clerk, earned a law degree, and held a number of elected offices, including mayor of Socorro at age thirty-one, county superintendent of schools, and district attorney for both Socorro and Sierra Counties.

After leaving public office in 1906, Baca became involved with Pancho Villa, the Mexican bandit-turned-revolutionary. They first conspired to lure a cattle thief who had fled to Mexico back across the border so Baca could claim a five-thousand-dollar reward. That plan fizzled when the reward was withdrawn. The two met again when Baca was working in El Paso. Villa asked him to smuggle some stolen goods into the United States. Baca agreed, but he had some trouble with border guards and showed up too late to catch Villa at a prearranged meeting. Villa accused Baca of misappropriating his property and threatened to kill him if he ever set foot in Mexico. Baca retaliated by arranging the theft of Villa's prized rifle; the revolutionary countered by placing a thirty-thousand-dollar price on Elfego's head. Baca allegedly tried to collect the money by setting up a fake capture, but it never happened.

In 1914, Baca was involved in another successful jailbreak. While acting as legal counsel for General Victoriano Huerta's counterrevolutionary army in Mexico, he was called upon to defend José Salazar, one of Huerta's top officers. Salazar was convicted of robbery in El Paso and sent to Albuquerque to stand another trial. After his transfer to New Mexico, Salazar escaped from jail by implementing a complicated plan that involved a mysterious woman and soldiers disguised as beet pickers. The woman scouted the area and drew a map that Salazar's rescuers would use to get out of town after they freed him. Toward evening on the night of

*A life-size statue of Elfego Baca stands near
the site of his heroic gun battle.*
ALEX SMITH PHOTO

the jailbreak, the woman made a phony burglary report that drew one of the jailers from his post. The "beet pickers," who were actually Salazar's staff members, quickly overpowered the remaining guard, released Salazar, and drove him by car to the railroad station where they boarded the train for El Paso.

While all that was going on, Baca was establishing an alibi by drinking with friends in a local saloon. But as the group headed for the station, witnesses claimed that Salazar leaned out of a window when his car passed the saloon and shouted, "Adios y gracias, mi amigo Elfego!"

Baca was arrested in connection with the jailbreak but was never charged. Despite that, authorities always considered him the mastermind behind it.

He returned to Socorro in 1919 and was elected sheriff. Rather than have his deputies scour the countryside for criminals, he turned to the honor system and had the county clerk write letters that stated:

> *Dear Sir: I have a warrant here for your arrest. Please come in by [specific date] and give yourself up. If you don't, I'll know that you intend to resist arrest, and I will feel justified in shooting you on sight when I come after you. Yours truly, Elfego Baca.*

The letter resulted in the arrest of every recipient except one. He wrote back that if Baca wanted him, he'd be waiting under a big cottonwood by the river, armed and ready for a fight. The sheriff went to the river, also prepared to shoot it out, but the alleged criminal turned himself in rather than square off against a man who had survived a thirty-six-hour battle against eighty gunmen.

Over the ensuing years, Baca rose in prominence all across New Mexico. He started a newspaper and called it *La Tuerca* (The Nut). Subscription rates were "two dollars a year to good citizens, five dollars a year to bootleggers and five dollars a month to prohibition agents."

He also became well known as a defender of the poor and the working man. While Baca was serving as sheriff, the city passed an ordinance that called for sixty-day jail sentences for anyone who had outstanding debts, even as little as ten dollars. When Baca was forced to arrest several men under the new law, he jailed them as ordered but then let them go home and find work so they could pay their bills. The district attorney angrily attacked him for showing such leniency. Baca retorted, "They ate too much and they're better off at home." The law was repealed a short time later.

In his later years, Baca befriended some of the cowboys who had made him a human target. One of them, Jim Cook, sent Baca a photograph of himself with the inscription, "To Elfego Baca in memory of that day at Frisco." Baca allegedly responded with a note that read: "Those were the great old days. Everything is very quiet now, isn't it?"

The colorful career of Elfego Baca ended with his death on August 27, 1945. He was eighty years old. Milligan's Plaza was renamed Reserve because it bordered the forest reserves of the adjacent Gila, Apache, and Cibola National Forests. A life-size bronze statue honoring his memory was placed in downtown Reserve in 2010. The accompanying plaque tells the story of the shoot-out and credits a local group of citizens for funding the sculpture.

Although it has fewer than five hundred permanent residents, Reserve is still the seat of Catron County, the state's largest county but one of its least populated, where elk outnumber humans by almost a fifty-to-one ratio. And its false-fronted buildings are reminiscent of its past as a frontier town where one man stood up against a multitude.

CHAPTER NINETEEN
Pancho Villa's Raid:
An Unfamiliar Defeat in Familiar Territory

The town of Columbus, New Mexico, has the unique distinction of being a National Historic Site because it is the scene of the last foreign invasion of the continental United States. This southern New Mexico town also has a state park dedicated, oddly enough, to the leader of the invasion.

The invasion occurred in the early morning hours of March 9, 1916, when Columbus was just a sleepy little border town of about four hundred souls. Pancho Villa, a notorious Mexican bandit and revolutionary, led the assault. The battle lasted less than two hours, and the invaders suffered heavy losses before they were beaten back into Mexico. With that one brief but bloody scuffle, Columbus became a historically important site.

Villa was well known on both sides of the border, both as a revolutionary army leader and an outlaw. He was born on June 5, 1878, on a large hacienda in the state of Durango and named José Doroteo Arango Arámbula. His parents worked in near-servitude on the hacienda, and since Doroteo was the eldest of five children, he had to help his mother care for his siblings by taking work as a sharecropper after his father died. He left the hacienda at age sixteen but rushed back on hearing that Agustín López Negrete, the owner of the hacienda, allegedly raped Doroteo's sister. The vengeful older brother shot and killed Negrete, stole a horse, and fled into a mountainous area where he joined an outlaw gang headed by Ignacio Parra, one of the most feared bandits in Mexico. That one act of retribution led to a life characterized by rebellion and aggression.

During that time, Doroteo went by the name Orango Arámbula, and as Orango he was arrested for stealing mules and assault. He was initially given a death sentence but was spared and forced to join the army. That didn't work out well. Within months, he deserted, fled to the neighboring state of Chihuahua, killed an army officer, and stole his horse. He also changed his name to Francisco Villa in honor of his paternal grandfather, Jesus Villa. Eventually, Francisco became shortened to Pancho, the name he bore until death, although his associates also called him La Cucaracha (the cockroach).

He then organized a small ragtag army and launched a campaign of robbery and murder, partially redeeming himself by distributing his loot among poor farmers. His notoriety soon came to the attention of men who were planning a revolution against the government of Porfirio Díaz. They enlisted Villa to lead an army in support of Francisco Madero. Villa performed admirably but left the group after a dispute with another commander. Madero was eventually installed as president but was soon caught up in another revolution, this one against him. Villa returned to action, again gathering troops to fight for the Madero cause. But in June 1912, Villa was accused of horse theft and threatened with execution. A reprieve from Madero saved him from the gallows, but he spent almost seven months in jail before escaping.

In February 1913, Madero was killed by General Victoriano Huerta, who installed himself as president. Since Huerta made the accusation that sent him to jail, Villa allied himself with Venustiano Carranza to fight Huerta. His troops captured substantial portions of northern Mexico, and Villa became a sort of folk hero, dividing up conquered estates among the workers who had been in near-servitude to the big landowners. But then he and Carranza had a falling-out, which resulted in a state of near civil war between the two factions. And that indirectly led to the attack on Columbus.

The United States entered the fray and sided with Carranza, a move that infuriated Villa. He began planning the invasion as a retaliatory move.

Although the Mexican revolutions were raging just a few miles south, the residents of Columbus felt relatively secure because the

US Army had stationed about 350 soldiers from the Thirteenth Cavalry at Camp Furlong, located between the town and the border. Since the troopers had seen no action since arriving, Villa was counting on stealth, complacency, and surprise.

Around 1:00 a.m. on March 9, five hundred to six hundred revolutionaries known as "Villistas" rode their horses across the border at the Mexican village of Palomas and silently took up positions southwest of Columbus. As they waited in the dark, Villa repeated his orders that they were to raid, not kill. He wanted to send a message to Washington, D.C., not erase a community.

Villa's plan was not overly complex. He divided his men into two groups. Half would storm the town; the rest would stay behind with Villa and set up machine guns that would drive back the fleeing residents.

The attack began around 4:20 a.m., when Villa gave the order: *"Vayanse adelante, muchachos"* ("Go get 'em, boys"). As he had envisioned, the soldiers and townspeople were taken by complete surprise. The horsemen stormed into town, screaming and shooting. The gunfire, the shouts of *"viva Villa!"* coupled with the sounds of shattering glass and splintering wood created immediate chaos.

But not everyone panicked. Army Private Fred Griffin, a sentinel at Camp Furlong's regimental headquarters, saw the raiders and issued a challenge. He was shot down by a hail of enemy gunfire but managed to kill three raiders before he died.

While some Villistas concentrated on taking the army camp, others tore through the streets of Columbus, bent upon destroying the entire downtown. They set fire to some businesses and shot up others. One of their prime targets was Sam Ravel's commercial establishment. Months before the raid, according to local historians, Villa had ordered ammunition from Ravel and, although it was paid for, the shipment was never delivered. Another version said that Ravel made the delivery but the bullets were blanks. Either way, Villa was determined to have his revenge. He ordered his men to go to Ravel's home and capture him, then take him

Pancho Villa once led an unsuccessful raid into New Mexico.
SCOTTSDALE CC SOUTHWEST STUDIES

to his store to open the safe and give them the money Villa figured he had coming. Then they were told to kill him. But Ravel
was not home, so the raiders took his fifteen-year-old son Arthur
to the store. Once there, they ordered him to open the safe, but
he didn't have the combination. Frustrated, the outlaws tried to
shoot the lock off. But their bullets caromed off the steel safe and
ignited cans of gasoline sitting nearby. Arthur escaped, but the
store burned down.

As the assault raged, many residents fled from their homes
into the surrounding desert, but others fought back. They armed

themselves and began returning fire. The troopers at Camp Furlong also responded. They smashed locks to get weapons from the
armory and scrambled to put their machine guns ready.

From then on, it was a litany of brutality and heroics.

Lieutenant James Castleman left his barracks, shot and killed one
invader, organized the soldiers, and began a counterattack. Deploying
his troops amid heavy gunfire, Castleman mobilized his own unit and
soon turned back the right flank of Villa's army. Then he moved his
force into Columbus and took command of the main streets.

Sergeant Harry Dobbs was assigned to hold the line while
Castleman moved the rest of his troops into position. He did as
commanded. Although seriously wounded, he continued firing
until he died from a loss of blood.

Simultaneously, Lieutenant John Lucas leapt from his bed,
raced barefoot through the gunfire, and mobilized the machine
gun troop. He led his unit into the business district where they
found the Villistas silhouetted against the flaming buildings, making them easy targets for the machine guns and the rifles of Castleman's men. The invaders were caught in a deadly cross fire.

Meanwhile, back at the camp, the post kitchen and stable
crews waged their own brand of warfare. They attacked the Mexicans with boiling water, axes, shotguns, and anything else available. One raider met his end at the hands of a soldier armed with
a baseball bat.

While all that was going on, the invaders set fire to the Columbus Hotel, killed William Ritchie, the owner, and threw his body
into the flames. Several hotel guests escaped through the back
door, but John Walker and Dr. H. M. Hart were gunned down as
they ran out the front door. Charles Miller, the local druggist, died
while trying to get rifles from his store. Milton James and his
pregnant wife, Bessie, tried to reach safety behind the thick adobe
walls of the Hoover Hotel. They were shot and killed near the front
of the building.

Stephen Birchfield, another resident of the hotel, saved his
own life by writing personal checks made out to his assailants.

Arthur Ravel, still in his underwear after being dragged to his father's store, escaped when his captors were killed by army gunfire. He fled into the desert, scantily clad and barefoot, and ran for nearly three miles before stopping.

The unexpected resistance from both the army and the locals quickly dampened the Villistas' enthusiasm. Less than two hours after it started, the attack collapsed and the invaders were fleeing across the border. With the retreat turning into a full-scale abandonment of the cause, Major Frank Tompkins took command of two cavalry units and set out in pursuit. In the running battle that followed, his men reportedly killed as many as seventy-five bandits and wounded several more. Tompkins ignored boundary lines; he chased the Villistas well into their own country before calling off the pursuit when the troops ran out of ammunition. They returned without suffering a single casualty.

After sunrise, the villagers were able to survey the damage. Their town was devastated; smoke was still rising from the burnt-out buildings. Ten soldiers and officers were dead; so were eight civilians. The wounded included two officers, five soldiers, and two civilians.

While rounding up the surviving Villistas, soldiers discovered that some of them were mere children. One was a twelve-year-old who had been assigned to take care of the outlaws' horses. He was injured in the battle, so the troopers bandaged his wound and gave him morphine to ease the pain. He told his interrogators that he had been frequently beaten and pleaded for his life because the bandits had brainwashed him into believing that capture meant certain death at the hands of the gringos.

In a story about the interrogation, the *Deming Headlight* reported:

> *As the shadows lengthened the little bandit spoke only in soft short sentences, the morphine was doing its work, he was almost asleep, but he roused himself and said, 'Me bueno muchacho' [I am a good boy]. He was asleep. Pancho Villa has very, very much to answer for to his God.*

After the shooting was over, resident Sara Hoover described it in a letter to her brother:

> *Our soldiers and our citizens never dreamed that Villa would cross the border to murder innocent women and children. They think he might cross to steal horses and cattle, and our soldiers were scattered along the border. Our people think Villa has had spies here who have kept him informed of the troops along the border, and he could safely cross the line and murder a lot of American citizens, which would bring on war and unite the Mexicans. He must have known that in the end, the Mexicans would be defeated, yet he would hold a high place in Mexican affairs. ... There will be no war and Villa will be hunted down as a bandit and murderer and will lose his life.*

Villa had been badly beaten. He lost as many as one hundred men in the battle, and several others were taken captive and hanged by the army. His prized machine guns had to be left behind. Many of his horses were killed, and his troops had expended most of their ammunition during the onslaught. Even worse, perhaps, the US Army was about to become fully engaged in the situation.

On March 15, less than a week after the attack, President Woodrow Wilson ordered General John J. "Black Jack" Pershing to lead an army of forty-eight hundred men into Mexico and capture Villa. The large force, which became known as the Punitive Expedition, was equipped with a variety of new weaponry, including a Curtiss "Jenny" airplane and several mechanized vehicles. The expeditionary force had its first encounter with the Villistas on March 29 in a battle at the Mexican village of Guerrero. It was an American triumph, from a military standpoint. Villa lost at least another seventy-five men and was forced to retreat into the mountains.

There were other skirmishes, but Villa was never captured, despite the overwhelming number of soldiers looking for him. According to some reports, the bandits eluded the army by following them in the dust clouds being kicked up by the motorized vehicles. One legend, still popular in Mexico, says that Villa disguised himself as a peasant and walked into Pershing's camp unrecognized.

Most of the force was ordered withdrawn by January 1917, and Pershing bitterly complained that President Wilson had imposed so many restrictions on him that success was virtually impossible. He later wrote that "when the true history is written, it will not be a very inspiring chapter for school children, or even grownups, to contemplate. Having dashed into Mexico with the intention of eating the Mexicans raw, we turned back at the first repulse and are now sneaking home under cover, like a whipped cur with its tail between its legs."

But the expedition did serve another purpose: It allowed the army an opportunity to test its officers, its troops, and its new arsenal, a factor that played a major role when the United States entered World War I. And, although they never caught him, Pancho Villa was never again a threat to the United States. After Carranza was assassinated on May 20, 1920, Huerta was named interim president. In an effort to bring some calm to his troubled nation, he offered Villa a hacienda in his home state of Chihuahua if he would give up his life as a revolutionary and retire. Villa accepted, but his retirement was brief. He was gunned down in his car on July 20, 1923.

Historians still debate the reason behind the attack on Columbus. The most common theory is that Villa planned it in retaliation for President Wilson's support of Carranza and that he believed there was a conspiracy between Wilson and Carranza to make Mexico dependent on the United States. Others speculate that powerful oil companies and other interests wanted to install a leader who would favor American policies, so they opposed Villa.

And some believe the Germans were responsible. According to that line of thought, German interests preparing for America's possible entry into World War I hoped to create a distraction along the

*A larger-than-life bronze of Pancho Villa stands
in downtown Tucson, Arizona.*
VERA MARIE BADERTSCHER PHOTO

border to occupy American troops. To that end, so the theory goes, the German government had an agent infiltrate Villa's staff and convince Villa that the bank in Columbus had cheated him out of ten thousand dollars, angering the bandit enough to cause the attack.

Regardless of the reasons, the attack changed Columbus. There was an initial population explosion, caused by the need for troop services. National Guard units from Texas, Arizona, and New Mexico were called into service along the border on May 8. When Congress approved the National Defense Act on June 3, National Guard units from all the other states and the District of Columbia also were called into duty. At one point, 110,000 Guardsmen were deployed to the border, and that meant steady income for the residents of Columbus.

That all changed when the United States entered World War I, as emphasis shifted away from the border. Camp Furlong remained but only at a decreased level until 1926, when the Department of the Army shut it down. The closure hurt the town's economy, which took another blow in the 1950s when the railroads left town.

But the town endures. Now it has about eighteen hundred full-time residents who partially rely on tourism to boost the city's coffers. Many buildings involved in the Villa assault are still standing, some of them bearing the scars from that morning. Now, they're protected and cherished as part of Pancho Villa State Park, the only state park in America named after a former enemy.

Among the historic structures is the judge advocate's office and jail, formerly a part of Camp Furlong. The old jail bars are still intact, rather remarkable considering that the building was left to decay after the army pulled out. The Hoover Hotel also has survived the years. So has the Columbus school, where many women and children hid during the raid. It is still used as a learning center for children from both Columbus and Palomas, the Mexican village located south of the border some three miles away.

The park's centerpiece is a new museum, a seven-thousand-square-foot building that opened in 2006. It contains a full-scale replica of the Curtiss airplane used by Pershing's troops and a bullet-riddled piece of steel that was once part of the Dodge touring car that Pershing used as a field office. The old Customs House now serves as a visitor center for the park, which was created in 1961 and declared a National Historic Site in 1975.

Also on the grounds are huge sycamore trees that grew from seedlings presented to Columbus in 1946 by the state of Chihuahua as an expression of friendship.

Villa is doubly remembered in Palomas. A life-size bronze sculpture of the dashing bandit king rises over the small community plaza. It depicts him aiming his pistol while spurring his horse. Just down the street in a commercial plaza, there is another life-size bronze of Villa shaking hands with Black Jack Pershing.

Bibliography

PROLOGUE: THE LINCOLN COUNTY WAR

Bell, Bob Boze. *The Illustrated Life and Times of Billy the Kid*. Phoenix, AZ: Tri Star-Boze Publications, 2004.

Coe, George. *Frontier Fighter*. Albuquerque: University of New Mexico Press, 1934.

Fulton, Maurice. *The Lincoln County War*. Tucson: University of Arizona Press, 1968.

Keleher, William. *Violence in Lincoln County 1869–1882*. Albuquerque: University of New Mexico Press, 1942.

CHAPTERS 1 AND 2: BILLY THE KID: PART ONE AND PART TWO

Bell, Bob Boze. "Caught with His Pants Down?" *True West Magazine,* July 27, 2010.

———. *The Illustrated Life and Times of Billy the Kid*. Phoenix, AZ: Tri Star-Boze Publications, 2004.

Cahill, Frank. "Death Statement." *Arizona Weekly Star,* August 17, 1877.

Dodder, Joanna. "Officials Won't File Charges in Billy the Kid Grave Case." *Prescott Daily Courier,* November 6, 2006.

Garrett, Pat. *The Authentic Life of Billy the Kid*. Santa Fe: New Mexican Printing and Publishing Company, 1882.

Kutz, Jack. "Billy the Kid's Escape from the Grave." *Mysteries and Miracles of New Mexico*. Corrales, NM: Rhombus Publishing Company, 1990.

Lowe, Sam. "A Kid Named Billy." *New Mexico Curiosities*. Guilford, CT: Globe Pequot Press, 2009.

Nolan, Frederick. *The West of Billy the Kid*. Norman: University of Oklahoma Press, 1998.

Rojas, Rick. "N.M. Governor Won't Pardon Billy the Kid." *Los Angeles Times*, September 2010.

Trachtman, Paul. *The Old West: The Gunfighters*. New York: Time-Life Books, 1974.

Wallis, Michael. *Billy the Kid: The Endless Ride*. New York: W. W. Norton and Company, 2007.

CHAPTER 3: CHARLIE BOWDRE AND TOM O'FOLLIARD

Bell, Bob Boze. *The Illustrated Life and Times of Billy the Kid*. Phoenix, AZ: Tri Star-Boze Publications, 2004.

Charlie Bowdre's Grave. Find A Grave, 1998. www.aboutbilly thekid.com/young_guns_page_wg1.htm.

McAlavy, Don. "Tom O'Folliard: Loyal Friend to the End." *Billy the Kid Outlaw Gang* newsletter, 2005.

Nolan, Frederick. *The West of Billy the Kid*. Norman: University of Oklahoma Press, 1998.

Rasch, Philip. *Trailing Billy the Kid*. Stillwater, OK: Western Publications, 1995.

Utley, Robert. *Billy the Kid: A Short Violent Life*. Lincoln: University of Nebraska Press, 1989.

CHAPTER 4: BOB OLINGER

Gomber, Drew. "The Birth of a Legend, Part 2." *Alamogordo Daily News*, January 13, 2011.

Hough, Emerson. *The Imitation Desperado*. Legends of America, 1987. www.legendsofamerica.com/we-imitationdesperado.html.

Kelly, Bill. "Bob Olinger: New Mexico's Killer Deputy." Desert USA, 2005. www.desertusa.com/mag00/feb/papr/bob.html.

Officer Down Memorial Page, last post August 2010. www.odmp.org/officer.

"Wortley Hotel." The Innkeeper web site, January 1986. www.theinnkeeper.com/bnb/11486.

CHAPTER 5: WHISKEY JIM GREATHOUSE

"Billy the Kid: The Real Life (And Death) Story." Old Fort Sumner Museum brochure, 1998.

Kildare, Maurice. "Whiskey Jim Greathouse." *Real West Magazine,* Spring 1974.

Metz, Leon. "Whiskey Jim Greathouse." *Encyclopedia of Lawmen, Outlaws and Gunfighters*. New York: Facts on File, 2002.

"Standoff at the Greathouse-Kuch Ranch." Angelfire, 2004. www.angelfire.com/nm/boybanditking/pagewhiskeyjim.html.

CHAPTER 6: BRONCO BILL WALTERS

Harden, Paul. "The Last Train Robbery." *Socorro El Defensor Chieftain,* November 1, 2003.

Martin, Bob. "Train Robbers Stole More Than Money." KRQE-TV, May 20, 2009.

Melzer, Richard. "Robbers Roost." *Valencia County News-Bulletin,* June 18, 2011.

Tanner, Karen, and John D. Tanner Jr. *The Bronco Bill Gang*. Norman: University of Oklahoma Press, 2011.

CHAPTER 7: SHADY LADIES

Bell, Bob Boze. *The Illustrated Life and Times of Billy the Kid.* Phoenix, AZ: Tri Star-Boze Publications, 2004.

Marriott, Barbara. "Ada Hulmes: The Case of the Crazy Lover." *Outlaw Tales of New Mexico.* Helena, MT: TwoDot, 2007.

Tanner, Karen, and John D. Tanner Jr. *The Bronco Bill Gang.* Norman: University of Oklahoma Press, 2011.

———. "Murder and Scandal in New Mexico: The Case of Ada Hulmes." *Wild West,* December 2003.

CHAPTER 8: JOHN JOSHUA WEBB

Bennett, Charles. "Legendary Lawman JJ Webb." Officer.com, April 14, 2011. www.officer.com/article/10232786/legendary-lawman-jj-webb.

"John Joshua Webb." *Far West Magazine,* March 21, 2009.

"John Joshua Webb." Wikipedia, 2007.

Lacy, Ann, and Anne Valley-Fix. *Outlaws and Desperadoes.* Santa Fe, NM: Sunstone Press, 2008.

Robertson, Gary. "Las Vegas: Western Boomtown Frozen in Time." *Los Angeles Times,* June 1, 2011.

Weiser, Kathy. "John Joshua Webb: Lawman Turned Outlaw." Legends of America, March 2010. www.legendsofamerica.com/we-jjwebb.html.

CHAPTER 9: THE UNRECOGNIZED WORST OF THE WORST

The Complete List of Old West Outlaws. www.legendsofamerica.com/we-outlawindex.html.

"David Crockett y Gus Heffron." *The Daily New Mexican,* August 18, 1876.

Lee, A. L. "Black Landmarks in the Un-Black West." AfriGeneas Western Frontier Forum web site, July 24, 2005. www.ukv.edu/libraries/nkaa/record.php?note.

Marriott, Barbara. "Joel Fowler: Hanged for the Wrong Reasons." *Outlaw Tales of New Mexico,* Helena, MT: TwoDot, 2007.

"Offbeat New Mexican Ghost Towns." Brochure, New Mexico Tourist Attractions, 2010.

Turpin, Bob. *Rogues, Rascals and Scalawags of the Old West.* Grove, OK: Bob Turpin Publications, 2009.

CHAPTER 10: MILTON YARBERRY

Marriott, Barbara. "Milton Yarberry: A Shootin' Fool." *Outlaw Tales of New Mexico.* Helena, MT: TwoDot, 2007.

"Milton Yarberry." Wikipedia, date unknown.

Torrez, Robert. *Wild West in New Mexico.* New Mexico Department of Tourism. 2004–2011.

CHAPTER 11: JOSÉ CHAVEZ Y CHAVEZ

Hurst, James. "Hombre Muy Malo." Southern New Mexico Travel and Tourism, January 2003.

Index of Old West Gunfighters, 2010. www.legendsofamerica.com/we-outlawlist-s.html.

Marriott, Barbara. "Vincent Silva: The Man Who Fooled a Town." *Outlaw Tales of New Mexico.* Helena, MT: TwoDot, 2007.

CHAPTER 12: THE EXECUTION OF PAULA ANGEL

Lopez, Jesus. *Las Vegas History,* Program No. 6, for KFUN Radio. March 1, 2010.

Thwaites, Ernie. "Bizarre Frontier Hanging Recalled." *The New Mexican,* April 26, 1961.

Torrez, Robert. "Paula Angel: The Search for the Only Woman Ever Hanged in New Mexico." *New Mexico Law Journal,* 1981.

Wilson, Robert. "Executed Women of the West." *Big Blend Magazine,* 1998.

CHAPTER 13: CLAY ALLISON

Cleaveland, Norman. "Clay Allison's Cimarron." *New Mexico Magazine,* March/April 1974.

Myers, Roger. "The True Story of Clay Allison and Wyatt Earp." Ford County Historical Society, 2002. www.skyways.org/orgs/fordco/myers.html.

Sonnichsen, C. L. "Allison, Robert Clay." *Handbook of Texas Online,* June 2001. www.tshaonline.org/handbook/online/articles/fal39.

Weiser, Kathy. "Clay Allison: Colfax County Bad Boy." Legends of America, 2010. www.legendsofamerica.com/we-clay allison.html.

CHAPTER 14: MASSAI

Garfield, Brian. *Western Films: A Complete Guide.* New York: Rawson Associates, 1982.

"Massai." Wikipedia, August 16, 2011.

Paul, Lee. "Massai and the Apache Kid." Indian Legends, www.theoutlaws/indians3.htm.

Remington, Frederic. "Massai's Crooked Trail." *Harper's New Monthly Magazine,* January 1898.

Simmons, Marc. "Massai's Escape Part of Apache History." *The New Mexican,* November 2008.

Chapter 15: The Ketchum Brothers

Barton, Barbara. *Ruckus along the River.* San Angelo, TX: Anchor Publishing, 1997.

"Black Jack." New Mexico Department of Tourism, 2001.

Burton, Jeffrey. "Tom Ketchum and His Gang." *Wild West,* February 2002.

Lowe, Sam. "One Town's Answer to Billy." *New Mexico Curiosities.* Guilford, CT: Globe Pequot Press, 2009.

Maas, Nate. "Tom 'Black Jack' Ketchum." Nate's Nonsense web site, December 8, 2010. www.natemaas.com/2010/12/tom-black-jack-ketchum.html.

Ritter, Justine. "Thomas E. 'Black Jack' Ketchum." Bad Hombres, 2005. www.badhombres.com/outlaws/black-jack-ketchum.htm.

Chapter 16: Christopher "Kit" Joy

Alexander, Bob. "Guns, Girls and Gamblers." Desert Exposure, January 2007. www.desertexposure.com/200701/200701_true_west.html.

Bronson, Edgar Beecher. "The Evolution of a Train Robber." *The Red-Blooded Heroes of the Frontier.* London: A.C. McClurg & Co., 1910.

Bullis, Don. "The Kit Joy Gang Bites the Dust." Reprint of news story entitled "Will Rob No More," from *Albuquerque Morning Journal,* March 11, 1884. Reprinted in the New Mexico Historical Notebook, November 2, 2005.

Finn, Maria. "36 Hours in Silver City, N.M." *New York Times,* January 13, 2006.

CHAPTER 17: GEORGE MUSGRAVE

Alexander, Bob. "Desert Desperadoes." Desert Exposure, October 2006. www.desertexposure.com/200610/200610_desert_desperadoes.html.

Tanner, Karen, and John D. Tanner Jr. *Last of the Old-time Outlaws: The George West Musgrave Story.* Norman: University of Oklahoma Press, 2002.

CHAPTER 18: BAD BACA BOYS

Hardin, Jesse W. "Elfego Baca and the Frisco War." Legends of America, 2006. www.legendsofamerica.com/we-elfego baca.html.

Johnson, Byron A. "The Rousing Life of Elfego Baca." New Mexico Office of the State Historian. 2004–2011.

Lowe, Sam. "A Lawman's Long Day." *New Mexico Curiosities.* Guilford, CT: Globe Pequot Press, 2009.

CHAPTER 19: PANCHO VILLA'S RAID

"History of the Columbus Raid." New Mexico State University Department of Public History. Date unknown.

Lacey, Marc. "In the Echo of Pancho Villa." *Columbus Journal,* August 25, 2011.

O'Brien, Steven. *Pancho Villa.* New York: Chelsea House Publishers, 1994.

Sharp, Jay. "Pancho Villa Raids Columbus." DesertUSA, 2008. www.desertusa.com/mag07/feb07/villa.html.

Index

Rudabaugh, Dave, 35, 45–46, 47,
    70–71, 73, 75
Ruiz, Fernan, 176

S

Salazar, José, 184, 186
Sandoval, Gabriel, 102, 105, 106, 107
Santa Fe New Mexican, 58
Santa Fe Ring, 125, 127
Santa Fe Sun, 66
Sarracino, Pedro, 181, 183
Sawtelle, William, 164
Scarborough, George, 58
Scurlock, Josiah "Doc," 23–24
Sederwall, Steve, 20–21
Sena, José D., 115–16
Separ, NM, 53
Shaefer, George, 3
Shakespeare, NM, 82, 83–84
Sheehan, Edward, 66
Sieber, Al, 133–35
Silva, Emma, 102, 106
Silva, Jesus, 21
Silva, Telesfora, 102, 106–7
Silva, Vicente, 77, 102–8
Silver City, NM, 53–54, 55
Small, George, 79–80
Smith, Erichus "Rackety," 162
Smith, Walkalong, 19
Sociedad de Banditos (Society of
    Bandits), 103
Sociedad de Mutua Protección
    (Mutual Protection Society), 105
Socorro Sun, 178
Solomonville/Solomon, NM, 52
*Some Recollections of a Western
    Ranchman* (French), 183–84
Southern Pacific Railroad, 148,
    157–58, 170
Spencer, Charles, 161–62
St. James Hotel, 119, 126
Steck, Joseph, 45–46
Stevens, Charles, 52
Stockton, Isaac "Ike," 80–81
Stockton, Sam, 81, 83
Stockton, William Porter "Port,"
    80–81
Sullivan, Tom, 20–21

T

Tafoya, José, 44
Taggart, Frank, 157–58, 160, 162
Tattenbaum, William "Russian Bill,"
    83–84
Teats, Mary, 66
Thompson, Jim, 94
Tolby, Franklin J., 125
Tompkins, Frank, 193
True West, 141
Trujillo, Juan, 104–5, 106, 107
Tucker, Dan, 160
Tunstall, John, 5–6, 24

U

Upson, Ash, 12–13

V

Valdez, Antonio José, 107
Vega, Cruz, 125–26
Vigil, Francisco, 57
Villa, Pancho, 184, 188–98

W

Wade, E. C., 162–63
Wallace, Lew, 8, 9, 10, 12, 15–16
Walters, Bronco Bill, 50–60
Weaver, Bruce "Red," 149
Webb, John Joshua, 70, 71–73, 74,
    75, 76
Webster, Theophilus C., 157–58
Wells Fargo, 56–57, 58, 59, 60
White Caps, 103, 104, 107
Whitehill, Harvey, 53, 159, 160
Wilkinson, Burt, 81
Wilson, Billy, 35, 42, 44, 45–46, 47
Wilson, Woodrow, 194, 195
Woodland, James, 24
World War I, 197
Wortley Hotel, 39
Wuerro, Vicente, 57

Y

Yarberry, Milton, 90–98
Young, Code, 167–69, 172
Younker, Jake, 62

Z

Zanagoiiche, 140–41

About the Author

Sam Lowe has spent so much time in New Mexico, either researching material for books or simply enjoying himself, that he considers the state his second home. He has traveled more than ten thousand miles across the state and has yet to meet a grumpy person or an unattractive vista. Lowe has been writing about the Southwest for more than forty years. His previous book about the state was *New Mexico Curiosities,* also for Globe Pequot Press. He lives in Phoenix but goes to New Mexico every time even the slightest opportunity arises.

Author Sam Lowe
LYN LOWE PHOTO